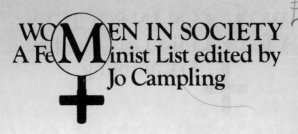

WOMEN IN SOCIETY
A Feminist List edited by
Jo Campling

editorial advisory group

Maria Brenton, *University College, Cardiff*; Phillida Bunckle, *Victoria University, Wellington, New Zealand*; Miriam David, *Polytechnic of the South Bank*; Leonore Davidoff, *University of Essex*; Janet Finch, *University of Lancaster*; Jalna Hanmer, *University of Bradford*; Beverley Kingston, *University of New South Wales, Australia*; Hilary Land, *Royal Holloway and Bedford New College, University of London*; Diana Leonard, *University of London Institute of Education*; Susan Lonsdale, *Polytechnic of the South Bank*; Jean O'Barr, *Duke University, North Carolina, USA*; Arlene Tigar McLaren, *Simon Fraser University, British Columbia, Canada*; Jill Roe, *Macquarie University, Australia*; Hilary Rose, *University of Bradford*; Susan Sellers, *Centre D'Etudes Féminines, Université de Paris*; Pat Thane, *Goldsmiths' College, University of London*; Jane Thompson, *University of Southampton*; Clare Ungerson, *University of Kent at Canterbury*; Judy Walkowitz, *Rutgers University, New Jersey, USA*.

The 1970s and 1980s have seen an explosion of publishing by, about and for women. This new list is designed to make a particular contribution to this process by commissioning and publishing books which consolidate and advance feminist research and debate in key areas in a form suitable for students, academics and researchers but also accessible to a broader general readership.

As far as possible books will adopt an international perspective incorporating comparative material from a range of countries where this is illuminating. Above all they will be interdisciplinary, aiming to put women's studies and feminist discussion firmly on the agenda in subject-areas as disparate as law, physical education, art and social policy.

WOMEN IN SOCIETY
A Feminist List edited by
Jo Campling

Published

Sheila Allen and Carol Wolkowitz   **Homeworking: myths and realities**
Jenny Beale   **Women in Ireland: voices of change**
Angela Coyle and Jane Skinner (*editors*)   **Women and Work: positive action for change**
Gillian Dalley   **Ideologies of Caring: rethinking community and collectivism**
Leonore Davidoff and Belinda Westover (*editors*)   **Our Work, Our Lives, Our Words: women's history and women's work**
Emily Driver and Audrey Droisen (*editors*)   **Child Sexual Abuse: feminist perspectives**
Diana Gittins   **The Family in Question: changing households and familiar ideologies**
Frances Heidensohn   **Women and Crime**
Ursula King   **Women and Spirituality: voices of protest and promise**
Muthoni Likimani (*Introductory Essay by Jean O'Barr*)   **Passbook Number F.47927: women and Mau Mau in Kenya**
Jo Little, Linda Peake and Pat Richardson (*editors*)   **Women in Cities: gender and the urban environment**
Sharon Macdonald, Pat Holden and Shirley Ardener (*editors*)   **Images of Women in Peace and War: cross-cultural and historical perspectives**
Shelley Pennington and Belinda Westover   **A Hidden Workforce: homeworkers in England, 1850–1985**
Vicky Randall   **Women and Politics: an international perspective** (2nd edn)
Rosemary Ridd and Helen Callaway (*editors*)   **Caught Up in Conflict: women's responses to political strife**
Patricia Spallone   **Beyond Conception: the new politics of reproduction**
Taking Liberties Collective   **Learning the Hard Way: women's oppression in men's education**
Clare Ungerson (*editor*)   **Women and Social Policy: a reader**
Annie Woodhouse **Fantastic Women: sex, gender and transvestism**

Forthcoming

Eileen Aird and Judy Lown   **Education for Autonomy: processes of change in women's education**
Niamh Baker   **Happily Ever After? Women's fiction in post-war Britain**
Jennifer Breen   **Women and Fiction**
Maria Brenton   **Women and Old Age**
Joan Busfield   **Women and Mental Health**
Ruth Carter and Gill Kirkup   **Women in Engineering**
Lesley Ferris   **Acting Women: images of women in theatre**
Tuula Gordon   **Feminist Mothers**
Frances Gray   **Women and Laughter**
Eileen Green, Diana Woodward and Sandra Hebron   **Women's Leisure, What Leisure?**
Jennifer Hargreaves   **Women and Sport**
Annie Hudson   **Troublesome Girls: adolescence, femininity and the state**
Susan Lonsdale   **Women and Disability**
Mavis Maclean   **Surviving Divorce: women's resources after separation**
Lesley Rimmer   **Women's Family Lives: changes and choices**
Susan Sellers   **Language and Sexual Difference: feminist writing in France**
Janet Wolff   **The Art of Women**

Fantastic Women

Sex, Gender and Transvestism

Annie Woodhouse

MACMILLAN

© Annie Woodhouse 1989

All rights reserved. No reproduction, copy or transmission
of this publication may be made without written permission.

No paragraph of this publication may be reproduced, copied
or transmitted save with written permission or in accordance
with the provisions of the Copyright Act 1956 (as amended),
or under the terms of any license permitting limited copying
issued by the Copyright Licensing Agency, 33–4 Alfred Place,
London WC1E 7DP.

Any person who does any unauthorised act in relation to
this publication may be liable to criminal prosecution and
civil claims for damages.

First published 1989

Published by
MACMILLAN EDUCATION LTD
Houndmills, Basingstoke, Hampshire RG21 2XS
and London
Companies and representatives
throughout the world

Typeset by Vine & Gorfin Ltd
Exmouth, Devon

Printed in Hong Kong

British Library Cataloguing in Publication Data
Woodhouse, Annie
Fantastic women: sex, gender and
transvestism. — (Women in society).
1. Transvestism
I. Title II. Series
306. 7'7
ISBN 0–333–44669–0 (hardcover)
ISBN 0–333–44670–4 (paperback)

Series Standing Order

If you would like to receive future titles in this series as they are published,
you can make use of our standing order facility. To place a standing order
please contact your bookseller or, in case of difficulty, write to us at the
address below with your name and address and the name of the series. Please
state with which title you wish to begin your standing order. (If you live
outside the United Kingdom we may not have the rights for your area, in
which case we will forward your order to the publisher concerned.)

Customer Services Department, Macmillan Distribution Ltd,
Houndmills, Basingstoke, Hampshire, RG21 2XS, England.

For my parents

Contents

Acknowledgements

Book-writing is a pretty lengthy process, and over the period of the production of this book and the research that went into it a lot of people have been involved in various ways. What follows is my thank-you list:

The transvestites at the TV/TS Support Group who welcomed me, answered my questions, invited me into their homes and teased me unmercifully about my appearance! All of this would have been much more difficult to accomplish without the support of Yvonne Sinclair (*'imself*).

The wives of transvestites who told me their life stories, recalling incidents and details which were sometimes painful to relate. The women in the Partners' Support Group at TV/TS who allowed me to attend their meetings.

Yvonne Webster, who battled with hours of interview tapes and got them on paper; and Debbie Jacques, who stayed cheerful when faced with innumerable requests for alterations.

Lots of people have looked at various drafts and provided me with much food for thought: Sara Bowman, Miriam David, Peter Davies, Rosy Fitzgerald, Dave King, Alice Lovell, Olive Leonard, Ken Plummer, Corinne Squire.

I am especially grateful also to: Dell Richards, for the effort and enthusiasm she put into knocking my writing into shape; Terry Relph-Knight and John Melmoth for patiently doing all the proof-reading and page-numbering; Brendan MacNeill for taking the cover photograph; Christina Dee for being the model.

ANNIE WOODHOUSE

Introduction

It's not often a book about men appears in a feminist series; still less so a book about men who spend their leisure time pretending to be women. Female impersonation has a long history and a wide currency; it confronts us frequently in the form of drag shows, fancy-dress parties and television comedy in the interests of entertainment and fun. But the notion that someone might take cross-dressing seriously and indulge in it privately and pleasurably provokes quite different reactions, more along the lines of the 'shock-horror' syndrome. But for every drag artist in the pubs and clubs there are many more men who like to dress as women, not for the entertainment of others, but for their own satisfaction. They are transvestites – men who derive pleasure, often sexual, always sensual, from creating a feminine appearance by putting on women's underwear, clothes, shoes, make-up and wig.

What does a fully clothed man look like? How would you describe him? Wearing trousers, shirt, a tie? But so do women. Short hair and no make-up? This is equally applicable to lots of women. It is a difficult question to answer, yet to all practical intents and purposes we 'know' what a man looks like. We expect men to dress to 'look like' men and women to 'look like' women. Thus to enter a room ostensibly full of women and to find that they are in fact men dressed and made up to resemble women is, at the very least, surprising. Imagine the effect of conversing with someone who looks and sounds female, who talks about her job as a receptionist in an all-female office, only to discover that 'she' is a 'he'. The revelation that a person's gender appearance is not a direct reflection of their biological sex is unexpected and can be disturbing. Sex, gender and appearance form a sort of trinity which runs deep in our social and psychological expectations of how our lives should be.

Quite simply, transvestism means cross-dressing – from the Latin 'trans' cross, 'vestire' to dress. It is not a single, unified process which is easily identified and categorised into convenient slots. To state simply that a transvestite is a person who cross-dresses is, in itself, insufficient, as this fails to identify the aspects which specifically characterise the transvestite. Not all cross-dressers are transvestites. There are drag queens, professional female impersonators, transsexuals and cross-dressed prostitutes, but the transvestite cross-dresses not for money, entertainment, politics, nor because he is convinced that he really is a woman. He does it from perceived need, often expressed as compulsion, and because he enjoys it. Transvestism represents a wholesale transgression of the 'rules' of gender in a manner which is both direct and extraordinary. It is socially proscribed and often controlled by legal sanction.

The ways in which we cling so tenaciously to 'appropriate' sex/gender linkages have been progressively clarified through the growth and influence of feminist politics and writing. The ways in which ideals of feminine beauty are constructed and maintained to coincide with men's interests have been well documented. What is less clear, though, is why some men should wish to take on these ideals of feminine beauty themselves to the extent of wanting to look like women and be accepted as such. Transvestite behaviour underlines an assumption which lies at the base of social interaction: namely that people who look like men are biologically male and people who look like women are undoubtedly female. More to the point, most people never even think about the assumption that men will *not* dress in women's clothes.

The transvestite is problematic because he dares to assume both genders. Biologically he is male and, for the most part, he will assume an 'appropriate' appearance, he will look masculine. This stands him apart from the transsexual who is convinced that he (or less frequently, she) is of the wrong sex and that the only way to rectify this imbalance is through surgery which will reassign him to the 'correct' sex. Transvestites are men. It is often argued, especially by transvestites themselves, that women do not experience a need to cross-dress because they can more or less dress to please themselves anyway. But transvestism includes a strong predilection for sexy, feminine underwear which sometimes includes wearing it under normal masculine attire, and it would seem that this fetishistic element is absent from the ways in which women learn to view sexuality. When a woman 'cross-dresses', say by wearing a man's-style suit, she is not trying to be a man, nor does she expect to be taken for one. She is simply following a trend. When the transvestite cross-dresses he wants to be convincing, to 'pass' in public as a woman. Affecting an extreme masculine appearance can denote a woman's sexual preference; in contrast, the transvestite is usually heterosexual, often married.

But why should a man want to appear as a woman? Why should he wish to masquerade as a member of the second sex, a group dominated and oppressed by men? In the act of cross-dressing the transvestite momentarily upsets the primacy attributed to masculine appearance, but does this undermine gender divisions? Indeed, is the transvestite a proactive feminist? To date, the bulk of research into transvestism has been contained within the closed circuit of medical and psychiatric specialist journals. It focuses on transvestism in a way that places it squarely within the arena of sexual deviance, where it becomes part of the spectrum of psychosexual disorders requiring treatment, cure or prevention. The individuals featured in the case studies may well be atypical of transvestites in general; as a rule they do not come to medical or psychiatric attention unless they are disturbed or under some kind of family or legal pressure to seek it.

Behaviourist psychologists rely on electric shocks and nausea-inducing drugs; psychoanalysts talk about 'phallic women' and weak fathers; liberals call for tolerance and social reform. In this respect *Fantastic Women* is quite different, presenting the first feminist study of transvestites in Britain today. It is not an apologia for the much maligned transvestite; rather it concerns itself with the particular angles that transvestism can offer to the study of gender as a social construction. In other words, this study goes beyond the traditional individualising approach which limits itself to asking 'Why do they do it?' and moves on to a focus based on sexual politics and the power imbalances contained in the social construction of gender.

Studies of gender roles are usually concerned with women, with a much smaller area of research devoted to examining the male gender role, but transvestism presents a peculiar anomaly: the biological male who knows and accepts that he is male and yet experiences a need to dress in women's clothing. To consider transvestism in relation to gender divisions allows us to see gender as a reflection of power and the lack of power.

Within this feminist framework two areas are examined which

have received little or no attention in sociological research. First, although it has already been demonstrated that there is a relationship between clothing symbolism and sexual politics (Wilson, 1985), the continuing primacy of masculinity in western society suggests that the study of gender divisions and sexual politics must include a sociology of appearance. In transvestism especially, appearance becomes the primary target, the goal being the perfection of a feminine guise. In this sense the apparent is divorced from the real, which in turn raises issues concerning the interlinking not only of sex and gender, but of sex, gender and gender appearance. It is assumed that the external appearance indicates not only biological sex, but also a person's inward gender identity. Transvestism upsets this assumption.

Second, in this study the views of some women married to transvestites are heard. Traditionally transvestism has been approached from the standpoint of the practitioners, the clinicians, or both. The role of women as wives of these men has remained largely invisible, receiving somewhat cursory treatment in two American studies (Feinbloom, 1976; Talamini, 1982). In Britain their perspective has been totally ignored (see Woodhouse, 1985).

Fieldwork in clubs, bars and private homes provided opportunities to meet a broad spectrum of men who like to dress up as women. Of course, it could be argued that the transvestites depicted here are equally as atypical as those in the various clinical case studies, but the point is that the transvestites featured here were largely members of TV/TS, an organisation and social club for transvestites and transsexuals. They were there because they wanted to be there and they were observed as transvestites interacting socially with other transvestites, not with 'experts'.

Fieldwork can often alter the researcher's original intentions and ideas, and this study is no exception. It started off as an investigation into the unwritten rules of gender demarcation with the purpose of presenting the case that transvestism is one way of breaking down the barriers. Meeting Eleanor, the wife of a transvestite (see Chapter 6) changed this. Suddenly transvestism wasn't simply about men transgressing the rules of gender in private; it involved marriages and conflict and sometimes suffering. Interviews with other wives underlined this. It's always said that there are two sides to every argument and the intention here is to present these two sides, but total neutrality is not possible and sides have to be taken.

In this respect this is not a study which is particularly sympathetic to transvestism. Of course, some transvestites will argue that a woman cannot possibly understand transvestism, but this can only be self-defeating, coming from those who want to become temporary 'women', supported by understanding wives.

Chapter 1 examines the relationship of sex and gender and the idea of sex as a non-problematic biological distinction. The vast majority of people regard biological sex unquestioningly, seeing it as something natural and fixed. Gender is the cultural identification of femininity and masculinity. It is both announced and recognised through various visual and vocal signals: hair, clothes, body shape and movement, gestures and facial expressions, voice and speech. Like sex, gender is thought of as fixed: that people are either masculine or feminine and that this is wholly determined by the shape of their genitals and the function of their reproductive organs. The common assumption is that sex and gender fit, that gender appearance is an accurate reflection of biological sex. These unwritten laws of 'fit' are encapsulated in the social expectations we have about clothing and appearance. Clothing forms part of a system of social signalling; it is used to indicate belonging, status, occasions and events along with personal and social identity. Above all, it is used to demarcate gender, so that although the symbols change with fashion the gender/sex message remains the same, namely that feminine appearance indicates female sex and masculine appearance male sex. Clothing is a badge of gender status, thus 'correct' gender appearance reaffirms our belief in the mutual exclusivity of masculine and feminine. Transvestism offers a means of examining these conventions of gender.

Chapter 2 considers the problems of definition: the confusion with drag, with sexual direction and expression and the overlap with transsexualism. Transvestism involves wearing feminine clothing, but it goes beyond simple fetishism and encompasses gender identity and sexual desires. Its mainly privatised nature precludes accurate estimates of its extent, but a total of 30 000 transvestites in Britain has been suggested. Transvestite groups tend to claim higher numbers. The transvestites represented here may or may not be typical of the total – there is no way of knowing. The research base TV/TS, a meeting-place for cross-gendered men, is introduced along with members – the transvestites, transsexuals, the partners and the punters.

Academic convention requires that the researcher as a real and gendered human being disappears in the writing-up stage, and that 'the facts' are simply reported. Against such convention much of the section dealing with TV/TS is written in the first person, but with good reason. At the time of research it was unusual for a 'real' woman to visit the club, and almost unheard of if she wasn't partnering a transvestite. As far as I know, I am the first female sociologist to conduct such a study in Britain and undoubtedly my presence had an impact if only because of my sex. Although I was sometimes on the receiving end of unwelcome attention, I also had an advantage over a male researcher because the transvestites were keen to talk to me and ask advice about cosmetics and hairstyles, which paved the way for greater rapport. But above all else I was an outsider and I perceived the whole scene as such.

Chapter 3 explodes the myth of the typical transvestite and examines the diversity of transvestite lifestyles and ways of coping with a double life. Examples of differing experiences are related to age and the significance attributed to cross-dressing, from the leisure-time-only transvestite, to the full-time 'woman'.

Chapter 4 reviews the medico-psychiatric and psychoanalytical literature. The causes of transvestism have been attributed to a whole gamut of factors: biological, early childhood, oedipal conflicts and faulty socialisation. Medical models have proposed cures; psychoanalytical approaches suggest individual resolution; others call for prevention through correct upbringing. The ideas about what constitutes normality and abnormality are unspecified, thereby lending credence to traditional ideologies of gender and the notion of 'correct' gender role behaviour. On the basis of this failure to explain causes, it is argued that we may learn more from considering the social effects of transvestism and the responses to it.

Chapter 5 considers whether transvestism has a role to play in breaking down gender divisions. While some transvestites and transsexuals may argue that it does – and indeed Carol Riddell, a post-operative transsexual, makes a strong case for it as a weapon in the fight against patriarchy – feminist responses to it have tended to revolve around cultural feminism and an ensuing condemnation. Proponents of transvestism have promoted it as the means to psychic wholeness and a completion of the self; thus the possibility of an anti-sexist transvestism is raised. However, in turning to the existing research we find that in the case of transvestism in marriage it is often the wives who are expected to shoulder the blame, while their transvestite husbands are considered to be the real victims; hence the necessity of investigating wives' experience.

Marriage to a transvestite can raise problems associated with sexuality, clothing fetishism, sexual demands, money, children. This has been intensified by the lack of support systems for women in such marriages. In Chapter 6 the experiences of five such wives are reported in detail in their own words, providing a strong contrast with the views of the 'experts' outlined in the previous chapter and also with the views of many of the transvestites themselves. In Chapter 7 the help available to wives is discussed: the few publications directed at women married to transvestites and a recently formed partners' suport group at TV/TS.

Why then should transvestism matter? One of the difficulties here is that although the case for liberal tolerance can be made quite convincingly, unconditional acceptance of it would entail outright rejection of the experiences of the wives outlined in Chapter 6, and their need for support cannot be simply written off as a personal solution to a social problem. From a feminist standpoint, gender roles and gender identity raise issues of social control. Women are kept down and restricted through the patriarchal imposition of feminine ideals which is both the result of and a support for masculinity's retention of primary status in society. Such divisions stunt development and when young boys are taken to gender-identity clinics because they are failing to show the 'correct' gender behaviour we throw up our hands in horror.

But there are serious contradictions here for feminism. It is simply not enough to state that we must tolerate transvestites, all the while thinking, 'but I wouldn't want to live with one'. The fact of the matter is that a lot of women, feminists and non-feminists alike, want their man to *be* a man, and that most definitely does not include wearing dresses, high heels and make-up. Do we deny the validity of these feelings? It is concluded that the contradiction is more apparent than real. The claim for tolerance based on the assertion that transvestism blurs the edges of the gender divide is a false one. Transvestism is a form of fractured behaviour which compartmentalises masculinity and femininity; thus the possession of two wardrobes does not make for a more complete self, any more than it makes for greater sexual equality.

1

Seeing is believing? Sex, gender and appearance

'Vain trifles as they seem, clothes have, as they say, more important offices than merely to keep us warm. They change our view of the world and the world's view of us.'

(Virginia Woolf, *Orlando*)

What do we see in the first few moments of an initial encounter with someone? We see their sex – at least, we *think* we see their sex, but in fact we do not. What we see is their *gender appearance* and we assume that this is an accurate indication of their sex. Most people will feel completely certain of the biological sex of the majority of people they meet in their daily lives of work and leisure, they will feel sure gender appearance denotes biological sex; but they may be wrong.

Indeed it could almost be said that in the world of social interaction there is no such thing as 'just a person'. In other words, 'personhood' consists of all sorts of characteristics, so the individual comes to be recognised and communicated with on the basis of belonging to certain groups, or rather by being seen as belonging to certain groups. Membership of, or exclusion from, these groups is saturated with meaning. So when we initially see a person we see them through a framework: we don't think 'That's a person', we think 'That's a wealthy woman', or 'That's a black woman', or 'That's an old man' and so on. Thus appearances convey, in various and often subtle ways, the major hierarchies and social cleavages of modern society: sex/gender, racial division, class position.

1

2 *Fantastic Women*

Sex

If we are to tackle the complexities of gender and the ways in which
it is communicated to others, we need first to establish what sex is.
While it may be commonplace to state that sex refers to biological
differences, and gender to the culturally designed aspects of that
difference, it is unusual for the analysis of biology to be extended
further in this respect (leaving aside the claims of the socio-
biologists). But what exactly do we mean when we refer to
biological sex? Sex divides people into female and male and this is
generally considered to be a non-problematic distinction, unless
there is some congenital malformation. Sex is, for the most part,
fixed and unchanging, although of course this can now be altered by
hormonal therapy and surgical reassignment. Indeed, sex labelling
is highly significant; whenever a baby is born the first question
people ask is, 'Is it a girl or a boy?'

For the purposes of this discussion it may be useful to think of sex
as comprising a number of variables. Although they are usually
considered fixed for life, some may be amenable to alteration, with
various degrees of difficulty encountered in the process.

Biology	1.	Chromosomal sex
	2.	Gonadial sex
	3.	Hormonal sex and pubertal maturation
	4.	Internal subsidiary reproductive mechanisms
	5.	External genitalia
Culture	6.	Sex assignment
	7.	Gender role and orientation

The majority of people go through life without paying much
attention to these components of biological sex, unless perhaps
there is a problem requiring medical intervention. As a rule people
do not consider changing any of these components into those
associated with the opposite sex, unless they are transsexual.
Transsexuals feel that they 'really' belong to the opposite sex and
that they have been encumbered with the wrong body, and thus they
want what has become known as a 'sex change'. A transsexual
may be a female (wanting to be male) or male (wanting to be
female), although the latter are far more common. Prior to a 'sex

change' a transsexual will change gender role and orientation – looking and living, and possibly working, as a member of the opposite sex. The post-operative transsexual has changed sex in all but one component: gonads and internal reproductive mechanisms are surgically removed; hormones and external genitalia are chemically and surgically redirected and restructured; only chromosomal sex remains the same.[1]

In contrast, the transvestite does not attempt to change biological sex at all. He knows he is a man and does not wish to be female, but now and then he alters one cultural variable – gender role – by dressing up and creating the appearance of a woman. In attempting to analyse transvestism, then, we are looking at cultural factors, questions of gender rather than biological sex.

Gender

By virtue of being either female or male we belong to one of two groups which in western societies are differentiated by much more than physical characteristics alone. On a social and cultural level the two groups are mutually exclusive, and thus we acquire another level of identity – feminine or masculine – which is recognised by means of a massively intricate network of symbols. Of course, the content of these symbols varies tremendously over time and between cultures, but the forms they take are expressed through such factors as use of language, sexual behaviour, emotional expression and, most importantly, appearance – i.e. clothes, hairstyles, accessories, mannerisms, gestures, body movements, vocal intonation and so on. Now the interesting point here is that it is generally assumed that sex and gender fit together; that the appearance of femininity denotes female sex and the appearance of masculinity, male sex. This assumption is so deeply ingrained and so completely taken for granted that in the course of our everyday lives we rarely, if ever, think about it. It just does not occur to us that we do not know the sex of most people and that all we have to go on is appearance.

In many respects this is not as odd as it seems. The assumption of fit between sex and gender is just one of millions that we rely on continually to enable us to live our lives smoothly. Basically, we assume that people see things in more or less the same way as we do, not so much in terms of major concerns like politics or religion (here we are more likely to think that other people *should* see the world as we do), but more with regard to the minute details comprising daily life. Imagine, for instance, unloading your shopping from the trolley onto the checkout belt, only to be asked by the cashier what you think you're doing; or stopping at a newsstand, asking for your daily paper and being met with a blank stare. People who talk to themselves in the street are 'weird' because *everyone knows* that talking is an activity performed in conjunction with at least one other person. People who run around naked are 'disturbed' because *everyone knows* that you have to wear clothes in public places, with the exception of some beaches and saunas. Although usually taken for granted, daily life is a complex network of all those things that we 'know': the done and the not-done, how to behave and how to appear; in short, how to appear normal. Thus the man who wears wig, make-up, high-heeled shoes and a dress is very strange indeed. He is transgressing, even if only temporarily, the cultural component of the sex/gender link: the appropriate gender appearance assigned to the male.

When categorising a person as male or female we rarely know their biological sex, but such ignorance is not regarded as a problem precisely because it is assumed that sex and gender fit. Gender can be further divided into two aspects: gender identity (the private image), and gender role (the public image). Usually biological sex, gender identity and gender role will be congruent (and we will expect them to be so), but when incongruence occurs and becomes overt, social reaction can be harsh and censorious because this disparity shakes the very basis of the way the world works. As Money says, 'the conviction of most people [is] that their own personal experience of their own gender identity is the only true and proper one' (1974, p. 69). For the transvestite, then, his biological sex, his gender identity and his expression of gender role may come into conflict from time to time. Indeed, it is often the 'oddities' who perceive this most clearly. They have been forced to take one step back, as it were, to view themselves as other people see them in the attempt to perfect, or at least improve, their dissemblance. Jane Fry, a transsexual expresses this in her autobiography:

> If people can't put a label on you they get confused . . . People have to know what you are. You walk down the street and the first thing you do when you see a person is say to yourself, 'That's a

male. That's a female. That's an older person.' You categorise in your mind. One of the first things you do is determine the sex – if you can't do that it blows the whole system up.[2]

Feinbloom (1976) remarks that if the meanings of masculine and feminine changed, then possibly transvestism would disappear, a comment not infrequently made concerning the gender-divided state of affairs which prevails and has prevailed throughout written history. But simply to refer to changing the meaning of things through some unspecified mechanism smacks of a utopian dream world divorced from the realities of social practices and organisation. The contemporary meanings attributed to the cultural categories 'feminine' and 'masculine' are not free-floating or responsive to wishful thinking. They both respond to and influence some of the great power bases of western social organisation – the interrelated divisions of power, wealth and gender. Clearly the assignation of gender, as opposed to sex, in terms of appropriate behaviour, activities, clothing, language and gestures is neither an historical accident nor a cultural anomaly. It establishes a hierarchy whereby a sexual division of labour ensures an imbalance of power and control weighted heavily in favour of male supremacy.

Gender, then, is 'rigidly welded to the male–female dichotomy'[3] and, as such, the means of maintaining this bipolarity of gender are complex and subtle. It begins at birth and proceeds through processes of reinforcement, sanction and negation so penetrating that we are often unaware of the impact of our own and others' actions.[4] But gender roles do not exist as empty slots for us to fill, nor is gender identity stamped as some kind of printed circuit on the brain; we actively participate in the processes which construct and reinforce our consciousness of a gender-specific identity. Thus our subjectivity operates within gender-related channels, formed and structured by a world which is not of our making, a world which operates in the interests of those who hold the reins of power. It is often only through consciousness-raising that people become aware of, and thereby attempt to transcend, the rigidity and the restrictions imposed by the limitations of gender. Such transcendence will, of course, remain partial within present structures. Nevertheless, the tremendous advances made by women in identifying and communicating the gendered specificity of daily life cannot be dismissed.

But how, one may ask, does all this relate to the transvestite? The realisation that gender is not a fixed entity, that gender roles and expectations can be questioned, attacked and changed, emphasises the significance of viewing both gender roles and gender identity as social constructs whose meanings are continually affirmed and reaffirmed, negotiated and renegotiated through the social process of human communication and interaction. One assumption implicit in all this is that sex, gender role and gender identity will fit together, that they will exhibit a conformity to, and an identity with, either one pole or the other. Thus our ways of looking at things are not simply imposed externally, but nor are they entirely the products of individual minds. And while the expectation of conformity in general may be weak in many areas, the division of masculine and feminine is rigid and demanding, and carries punitive sanctions for those who go against the grain. While gender identity may be inward and private, its outward manifestation is gender role and appearance. When external signs fail to tally with social expectations, when they signify an identity which clearly contradicts biological sex, the sanction of the 'shock-horror' syndrome comes into force, sometimes accompanied by legal restrictions.

Deviation from this holy trinity of sex, gender and appropriate appearance is more likely to be tolerated in women, but such deviation when exhibited by men is viewed with horror. Women's appearance is stereotyped in the representations of sexuality and motherhood which saturate the media; nevertheless, divergence is tolerated to a degree. Women may appear in masculine-style clothing without immediate loss of status, provided that they remain identifiably feminine. However, outside of the closely demarcated boundaries of the drag act or the fancy-dress party, men cannot appear in *any* item of women's clothing without immediate loss of the superior status attached to the male and the full imposition of ridicule and censure. In short, the realisation that a person one thought was a woman is in fact a man can come as a shock.

To explain the greater degree of disapproval directed at men who wear women's clothes in comparison to women who wear men's clothes, we have to consider the sexual politics of gender. Femininity and masculinity are products of a social environment and the qualities attributed to these two categories have nothing timeless about them. Indeed, what is deemed to be appropriate in one time and place may be quite the reverse in another. The gender divide is not one of equal balance; the scales of power and control tip decisively to the side of masculinity, which is accordingly attributed primary status. Thus, to deviate from this status is to take a step down; to adopt the trappings of the second sex is akin to slumming it, or selling out. And those who protect and maintain the primacy of masculinity cannot allow this to happen or the whole edifice would crumble. But why should social reaction take the form that it does, and why should some men want to cross the Maginot Line of gender identity and role? One way to examine this is to consider how gender is communicated and interpreted in social life, especially the way clothing operates as a primary means of gender signalling. Additionally, the relationship of clothing to sexuality provides some insight into the fact that transvestism is a largely male phenomenon.

Announcing gender

Gender is the end result of a social process which assigns certain characteristics to the biological categories 'male' and 'female'. Such classification is made on the basis of observable features: clothing, hairstyle, facial features, body shape, mannerisms, voice, gestures. Generally speaking, it is an unconscious process. Rarely, if ever, do we pause to wonder if an individual is 'really' a man or a woman; rather, perception is immediate and simple because, although we may not have direct knowledge of a person's genital sex, we 'know' what a man or woman looks like. In short, gender appearance is a key factor in social communication.

This social communication, or interaction, is made up of two components: language and appearance. As Feinbloom tells us, 'Appearance is that part of interaction which serves to define identity' (1976, p. 88). Thus in language, for example, we have to know someone's gender before we know which pronoun to use. Gender appearance comprises a system of signals which conveys information about self and expectations, not simply at the level of the individual but as an individual reflection and interpretation of more generalised codes operating in society at large.

Many of the traditional limitations and boundaries circumscribing appearance have changed. All the same, the announcement of gender is as strong as ever. It remains an ingrained and basic component of social perception, with feminine and masculine being treated as possessing some sort of essential reality, despite the fact that contradictory notions of femininity and masculinity span an historical and cross-cultural spectrum. The assumed rigidity of these categories has been attacked by Brake: 'There is no recognition of the possibility that men may be socially women (or vice versa)' (1976, p. 184). But does this kind of gender-relativism offer an adequate solution? The key lies in Brake's use of 'vice versa' which implies a comparable frequency of the phenomenon among women, when it is, in fact, rare. He thereby evades the question of why so few women attempt to appear *as men* although they may wear masculine clothes.

Here then is a central component of gender appearance. Just as our ways of looking at ourselves and the world are influenced by gender, so our perception of gender is orientated towards the supremacy of masculinity. In language, objects are male until proven otherwise, whether they are people, animals or insects (with the notable exception of nuns, cows and ladybirds). Not surprisingly, language's twin component in social communication, appearance, is similarly masculine, with the category of feminine coming in second.

Despite this depiction of gender as a fluid, ascribed attribute and as a product of social interaction, we tend, in everyday transactions, to treat it as a fixed entity, an absolute which is easily identified because this is 'the way things are'. Gender becomes an idealised, frozen concept in people's minds, with transvestites themselves often accentuating this notion despite their direct involvement in creating an illusory gender appearance. Their frequent preference for the stereotypically frilly and feminine suggests an image which has little reality in the daily lives of most women. Brierley (1979) agrees that the transvestite's perception of femininity may well be idealised: the belief that he can achieve attention and admiration by wearing pretty clothes. However, Brierley fails to recognise that this is understandable, if not entirely logical, in the context of a culture in which women are judged on their appearance. Randell (1975) agrees that the transvestite often has a highly idealised notion of a feminine image, yet in an earlier article he treats femininity in a rigid manner:

> They [transvestites] enjoyed feminine tasks, helping their wives with cooking, housework and other domestic tasks, or *merely*

sitting around playing the feminine role. (1959, p. 1449, emphasis added)

Randell is working with a notion of the feminine role as a 'thing' which one can play – while sitting around – like a game of charades. But there is no intrinsic quality of gender itself; gender refers to the ways we apply information: the signals which we perceive, interpret, label and use in order to respond to and interact with another person.

Clothes and signals

Appearance is more than simply the physical, outward manifestation of gender. It both moulds, and is moulded by, a person's own sense of identity. It is a means of signalling to others a whole range of meanings about oneself, about the relationship of self and others, and about the expectations one has of others and what their expectations in turn might be. In short, appearance makes statements about what a person is (or would like to be) and about the groups that person identifies with. An example of non-visual communication provides an illustration of this. When contact with someone has only been by telephone or letter the first meeting frequently contains an element of surprise: 'She wasn't a bit like I expected. I thought she'd be much taller/shorter, fatter/thinner, older/younger . . . ' This is accentuated when gender appearance becomes an issue: for instance, on the telephone a transvestite may sound like a man, whereas in direct encounters the visual will sometimes dominate so that he becomes a convincing 'woman'. Dress, then, can be used to misinform. The undercover agent will dress according to the style of the group being infiltrated so as not to reveal true identity; the transvestite attempts to appear as a 'real woman'. But, of course, intention and interpretation do not always coincide; thus the agent's cover is blown, the transvestite is 'read' – seen as a man dressed as a woman.

To highlight the significance of appearance in social interaction, discussion here will focus primarily on clothing. Obviously the other components cannot be entirely excluded, but generally they tend to follow the image or style constructed and conveyed through the medium of clothes. Why are clothes so important? If they served only to fulfil the functions of protection and modesty (as suggested by early anthropologists), we would be hard pushed to explain the existence of the club tie or the stiletto heel, let alone the phenomenon of cross-dressing. Basic biological imperatives such as the need for food, shelter and warmth are socially moulded and mediated, and take on different forms in different cultures. Certainly the notion of human needs does not even begin to explain the vagaries and trends of fashion, nor does it explain the taboos placed on the wearing of certain items of clothing considered to be gender specific. Lurie (1983) contends that a basic function of dress is to distinguish sex as a biological imperative in order to ensure species survival, but, in fact, this rather simplistic claim is hardly borne out by the historical evidence. Wilson (1985) argues that clothing began to signify gender in a more distinctly exclusive manner in the opening years of the eighteenth century precisely at a time when socio-economic roles were being more clearly demarcated along gender lines. Additionally it was during that century that views about homosexuality underwent a change, from being considered an indulgence in depravity to an unalterable condition of the individual. In other words, a person could *be* a homosexual. This change underlined the necessity, Wilson argues, of signalling one's sexuality, clothing providing the appropriate vehicle. This interface between fashion and ideas notwithstanding, Wilson underestimates the gender specificity of clothes in earlier periods.

As a means of adornment, clothing operates as a code. That is to say, it is neither neutral nor meaningless, rather it is a way of saying something and is, therefore, a form of social communication. The meanings entailed in such communication, however, are not properties of the clothes themselves. We assign meanings to them and thus they come to mean something to us. Nor are such meanings fixed; indeed they can change according to context. The point here is that as Wilson has observed, 'In all societies the body is "dressed"' (p. 3). The meaning of clothes changes over time, sometimes radically, at other times more subtly and slowly. In pre-industrial Britain dress signified social rank, profession or trade; in modern times it has taken on more symbolic communicative and aesthetic roles, so that now 'clothes are the poster for one's act' (p. 242). In relatively short time-spans, however, similar 'posters' can come to signify different 'acts'. Some years ago a track-suit, for instance, would have been associated exclusively with sports participation; now it is everyday casual wear, found in chain-stores and designer shops, a monument to the growth of the 'democratic image' of modern woman.

We use clothes to speak our identity; or rather, our identities – because identity is not a unified and unitary phenomenon. We express personality through appearance, adopting different personae towards different people at different times. Clothing is used to signify a number of things: occupation or rank, a social setting, social status, sex/gender. It indicates occasion (work, a funeral, an exercise class) and the time of day (daywear, evening dress, sleepwear). How one 'looks' in part determines the responses of others: thus one can dress to look efficient and professional (the job interview), to look attractive and sexy (the party), or to affirm political credibility (the demonstration or rally). Clothing comprises a system of signs – in Lurie's terms, a non-verbal language which signals information to others, a process of which we may not be fully conscious but participate in all the same: 'I may not be able to put what I observe into words, but I register the information unconsciously; and you simultaneously do the same for me' (p. 3). We adhere to dress codes which, even when not clearly spelled out, act as markers for the boundaries of social groupings. Thus when confronted with formalised codes, we respond initially to the uniform rather than to the person: the police command authority through the medium of an identifiable uniform connoting state-legitimated power; the long black robes of the priesthood convey a totally different meaning from that communicated by the shabby denims of the convicted prisoner. Uniforms are used to symbolise authority and subordination, to camouflage individuality and to emphasise unity and discipline, to act as a visible badge of organisational affiliation.

The immediate impact of uniform depends on recognition – that is, people have to know what it means – but this is nothing more than a clearly stated formulation of the processes interwoven in the activities of everyday life. Some jobs require a high level of conformity to rules and a corresponding suppression of individualism; thus a uniform serves simultaneously to maintain the appearance of sameness and to submerge the person wearing it. This is then further elaborated into the various sub-strata of rank: for example, in the police or armed forces. Status is also conveyed through dress, sometimes in a compulsory manner, sometimes not.

The convicted prisoner may wear a distinctive outfit which is not his own, thereby accentuating the depersonalisation of someone who is a number before he is a name. The patient wears an anonymous hospital gown for examination, the nurse wears regulation uniform. Clothes can also be used to show status and wealth: the monogrammed belt buckle or silk scarf, for instance, indicates both. Note also how the status function of clothing enters into figures of speech: 'giving someone a dressing down' or 'defrocking a priest'.

Clothing expresses both individuality and group affiliation, but, more important, it mediates gender signals. We are left in no doubt of the fact by Langner (1959) who depicts clothing as a means of differentiating sex and thereby maintaining social order. For Langner, clothes literally make the man – even to the extent that he displays a remarkable degree of paranoia in the face of changing fashions which, he claims, are leading us to the very brink of social breakdown!

the invention of the trouser and the skirt has enabled western men and women to achieve a balanced social and sexual relationship over the centuries which, if greatly disturbed, may produce some highly unexpected results. Not the least of these may be the male's loss of his dominating position in most of the fields where he now holds sway . . . And men, hold on to your trousers, or you may end up wearing skirts! (p. 70)

Leaving aside the misogynist hysteria of Langner's exhortations, there is contained here a pertinent indication of the significance of gender-specific clothing: that gender difference is not simply a marker of sex difference, rather it symbolises the nature of gender status in day-to-day, visible form. In this sense Langner is right to suggest that 'correct' gender appearance both manifests and bolsters the status quo. When women obtained the vote the whalebone corset fell from favour; several decades later the media hyped bra-burning as symbolic of the Women's Liberation Movement.

While dress designates social position in terms of wealth and standing, it also acts as a means of sexual display. It has often been suggested that in the animal world, and also in the human world of the past, the male is the peacock. Only latterly has this display become reversed in the social arena. However, such claims avoid the fact that the peacock-style display has always been rendered by the male *as a male*; so, to argue, for example, that Louis XIV wore make-up and stockings is to miss the point. Deviation from temporal and social conventions of gender-appropriate dress was, and is, liable to sanction. What those conventions are is less important than the fact that they uphold and reflect the inequality of gender.

Wilson sees modern fashion as engaging in play with the boundaries of androgyny. 'Fashion permits us to flirt with transvestism, precisely to divest it of all its danger and power' (p. 122). But in fact this is only a partial truth. She fails to distinguish between the differential statuses attached to gender-specific clothing and contradicts a point made earlier in her book when she observes that, although fashion is irrational, it speaks to feelings of solidarity and group norms so that 'deviations in dress are usually experienced as shocking and disturbing' (p. 6). Wilson cannot have it both ways. Either we are permitted to deviate in dress or we are not. As it is, western culture is phobic about 'effeminacy', and thus by wearing an item of female clothing a man defines himself as a transvestite, a sexual deviant. On the one hand, he is resorting to the accepted means of creating and presenting an image through dress and, on the other, abrogating the 'rules' of masculine and feminine dress codes. Women, in contrast, can and do adopt masculine-style clothes. The acceptability of a masculine edge in women's wear combines the paradox of comfort, efficiency *and* sexual allure. Lurie remarks that when Diane Keaton launched the 'Annie Hall' look, women adopted a more relaxed image which contrasted with notions of a mysterious femininity, but in terms of a serious attempt at equality the look had little impact. With its image of a kid dressing up in her big brother's clothes, we are reassured that really the woman is only playing.

Feinbloom suggests that the reason that women are allowed to half dress (i.e. wear some items of male clothing), and men are forbidden to, lies in the gender specificity of status, that 'aspiration to female status is perceived as a "step down" ' (p. 251). Certainly her reasoning accords with the stricter parameters of male socialisation, the pejorative use of the term 'sissy' and the approval of 'tomboy',[5] 'Why else', asks Feinbloom, 'would some parents punish boys by forcing them to wear girls' clothing?' (p. 251). This preservation of superior status through the outwardly visible mechanism of clothing has also been recognised by Newton (1972) in her study of female impersonators in the United States:

> Even one feminine item ruins the integrity of the masculine system: the male loses his caste honour. The superordinate role in a hierarchy is more fragile than the subordinate. Manhood must be achieved and, once achieved, guarded and protected. (p. 101n).

In part, then, we can say that the rigid demarcation of clothing along gender lines in western societies facilitates the protection and recognition of a superior, masculine status – a visible and outward sign of supremacy. Indeed, when women do wear masculine-style fashion this can also confer touches of masculine status too; as Lurie comments: 'When women put on men's clothes they usually take on considerable dignity, and sometimes great elegance and sophistication' (p. 244). In reverse, the man who wears feminine clothing announces his deviancy, his demise as a male and his fall from the grace of superiority.

But clothing cannot be seen solely as a gender-signalling device. It can also, in certain contexts, be seen as a means of sexual signalling. An obvious example of this is the prostitute who, working on the street in the rain, would not don waterproof anorak and galoshes. Clothing conveys varying degrees of sexiness; sensible boots are not sexy, thigh-high leather ones are; nylon anoraks are not, fur jackets are, and so on. Eroticism is not an inherent property of clothing: any item could be defined as erotic. The point is that the association of sex and clothing pertains far more to women's clothes than to men's. That is to say, women are not turned on by items of male apparel – the sock is not the equivalent of the stocking – and the woman clothing-fetishist is an extreme rarity, if not actually non-existent. The structuring of sexuality takes on divergent meanings depending on gender, and we find that the wish to dress entirely in the clothes of the opposite sex is a practice confined almost entirely to men.[6]

So far the restrictions moulding gender appearance have been discussed in general terms, but a comment on appropriacy is needed. In other words, social setting plays a crucial role in the assignation and comprehension of clothing symbols. For example, compare the clothing worn to a formal dinner party with that appropriate for a casual supper. People dress to show that they belong to certain groups and to signify to others that they fit in with (or refuse to identify with) a particular group or sub-culture. Indeed, deliberate scruffiness, based on choice, can signify as much as elegance. Social convention and often tradition dictate the appropriateness of dress codes in specific contexts. Thus the bride does not wear black and the formal-dinner-party guest does not wear jeans. But we also know that the bride and the dinner guest in the long gown are female – or do we? In another context, such as a drag show, we would actually expect, and know, that the elegant 'lady' was male. Within closely confined limits, men are permitted to pose as women and may even be applauded for it. But to transgress those limits is to run the risk of not only social disapproval, but also legal complications and all that this entails.[7] Garfinkel (1967) remarks that when movement from one 'sex status' to another is permitted it is accompanied by definite controls, and that play-acting or fancy dress *must* be followed by a return to what one 'really is'.

Cross-dressing, then, is not deviant in and of itself but only when the reason for its occurrence is not deemed 'legitimate'; that is, when time, place and audience are inappropriate. Thus a particular action or appearance will mean different things in different situations. While a man dressed as a woman will be considered quite acceptable and normal at a drag ball, the context of the geographical distance between his home and the ball's venue may well render his appearance 'abnormal'. Indeed, even within the privacy of his own home the transvestite may be aware of a potential audience and the ways in which this can change the situation: for example, dressing as a woman and then answering the door to an unsuspecting neighbour.

In some respects it might be said that transvestism is behaviour that is labelled as such, so that it is just a change of context which causes the entertainment of the drag act to become sexual per-version. However, this sort of relativism leaves us none the wiser when attempting to isolate and define cross-dressing which is performed not for entertainment and financial gain but for personal satisfaction. The transvestite usually sees himself as someone who acts in response to some sort of compulsion. He experiences a need to transgress the limits of gender appearance to such an extent that there are times when his gender identity stands in complete opposition to his biological sex. Given the strict demarcation of gender appearance in this society and the stringency of dress codes applied to men in particular, it is only to be expected that many transvestites will experience feelings of guilt in relation to their activities. Some transvestites come to terms with their desire to dress in women's clothing, but sometimes only after considerable strain, self-doubt and even total breakdown.

That this activity should impose such conflict and yet be maintained and practised, often throughout a person's life, bears testimony to the extreme significance attributed to types of clothing by some transvestites. Why then, we may ask, do they do it? Approaches to these questions are multiple, varied and often contradictory, providing, if nothing else, examples *par exellence* of the ways in which preconceptions and prejudices inform and structure our ideas and expectations of the relationship between sex, gender and gender appearance. That these three components do form a unity, a holy trinity, in everyday attitudes and actions is underlined by both transvestites who transgress these social 'laws' by throwing the 'normal fit' of sex and gender into reverse, and by social reactions to their behaviour.

2

Through the looking glass

Defining transvestism

Despite the fact that cross-dressing has been found to exist throughout history, the term 'transvestism' was not coined until the early part of this century. It was not clearly differentiated from transsexualism as a clinical category until the 1960s.[1] Consequently there has been, and still is, a confusing muddle of terminology which links transvestism with transsexualism, homosexuality, fetishism, masochism and gender dysphoria – discomfort with one's appropriate gender identity. Such confusion does not provide any sort of accurate reflection of the ways in which the transvestite defines himself and his world. Rather it stands as an indicator of the different paths taken by ideas about sexuality, and particularly so-called deviant sexuality. These ideas moved from the behaviour modification models of the early and mid-1960s, into notions of social delinquency with its associations of inadequate parenting/ environment/childhood development, and on to the moral relativism which characterised the 1970s and is now under attack from the 'moral right'.[2]

If such lack of clarity and definition abounds among clinicians, psychiatrists and therapists – in short, the 'experts' – we may well expect to find an even greater welter of confusion running through popular thinking on the subject. Certainly the transvestite tends to be confused with the transsexual and/or the homosexual, the stereotyped expectation being that any man who wishes to take on the appearance of a woman really wants to do this on a permanent basis and is, therefore, something less than a 'real man' – he is 'effeminate' and thus a homosexual. To the despair of those who would attempt to categorise transvestites into neat and tidy compartments, the transvestite in fact presents many variations on a theme: he may be heterosexual, homosexual or bisexual; married, single or divorced; an occasional cross-dresser or virtually a full-time 'woman'; or rarely, he may decide that he is, after all, transsexual and desire sex reassignment surgery. In the interests of unravelling this tangle it will be helpful to consider some of the terms and the ways they will be employed in this account.

The transvestites referred to here are men. It is often claimed that there are no female transvestites because women can more easily wear masculine clothing. While this does, at least superficially, seem plausible, as an explanation it is undeniably time-bound, paying no heed to historical precedents. Suffice to say that although there have been women who dressed as men in the past, and even convinced others that they were men, this was either to facilitate their participation in activities which were open only to men (such as being a soldier or a sailor) or to connote sexual preference. However there is no evidence, then or now, of fetishistic cross-dressing by women, the derivation of sexual pleasure from wearing certain garments or fabrics. Male dress was adopted for practical reasons. As Stoller (1982) points out, female transvestism is largely a non-issue as it is extremely rare. He reports only three cases, one of whom was personally known to him, another with whom he had corresponded, and a third (probably transsexual) documented in the literature some fifty years previously. Redmount's account (1953) of a female transvestite in fact fits the criteria for transsexualism. During research I encountered only one woman dressed as a man, a transsexual who was waiting for sex reassignment surgery. The term 'transvestite' may be taken to refer to men dressing as women.

The term 'cross-dressing' covers a wide variety of activities such as theatrical burlesque, drag and camp, but perhaps the primary issue dividing these forms of dressing-up from transvestism is the element of masquerade. For instance, the drag artist, while creating a semblance of femininity, will never allow his audience to forget his true sexual identity, thus we know that such performers are men, enacting in one way or another a parody of femininity, often in a misogynistic manner. In contrast to this, the transvestite makes no attempt at satire; his ideal is to 'pass', or be seen as a woman, often deriving sexual satisfaction from wearing feminine attire. In practice, however, this distinction tends to blur, particularly at social events, so that the drag ball, for example, will often comprise aspects of theatrical drag, gay burlesque, gender-bending, transsexual 'women' and transvestites. Similarly, the transvestite may earn his living as a drag artist.

Kirk and Heath (1984) conclude from their pictorial study of men who cross-dress – drag artists, transvestites and transsexuals – that while the dividing lines are often blurred and that self-definition of 'what' one is can change over time, in comparison to drag, 'transvestism is generally a more serious business for those concerned' (p. 72). The transvestite experiences a confusion of gender identity which is not generally characteristic of the drag artist who cross-dresses primarily to earn a living.

At times the closely confined restrictions placed upon masculine appearance have been challenged by camp imagery, but these tend to be along the lines of wearing something 'feminine', one or two items of clothing, rather than full cross-dressing. Overall, drag, burlesque and partial cross-dressing intended as a political statement can all be grouped under the heading of performance, a long way from the private obsession of the transvestite. The illusion and fantasy of the 'gender fuck' protagonists of the 1970s – David Bowie, Alice Cooper and the New York Dolls – gave way to the poseurs and the gender-benders of the 1980s and the increasingly common use of make-up by musicians; but this, of course, does nothing for the transvestite who has no desire to emulate the image of men in make-up; the transvestite wants to pass, from time to time, as a woman.

On the other hand, the line dividing transvestism and transsexualism tends to be more complex and becomes confusingly hazy in some instances. We find that some sort of continuum exists when, albeit rarely, the periodic cross-dresser decides that he is transsexual. But even here the question arises, was he really transsexual all along but refused to recognise or accept the possibility? Perhaps a more easily recognisable point of departure would be to consider the transvestite as a person who identifies himself as a man-who-dresses-as-a-woman. In contrast, the transsexual will identify himself as a woman who has the misfortune of a male body; the solution being, in his terms, hormone therapy and sex reassignment surgery. In referring to the importance of changing genital sex, April Ashley, a post-operative transsexual, comments that as a biological male, 'my genitals were quite alien to me'.[3] Typically, the transvestite will display the opposite attitude, enjoying the best of both worlds.

In a social context, at clubs, the distinction tends to be much less clear, with transvestites and transsexuals mixing both socially and sexually as biological males and social females. This mixing also poses a further difficulty for those who would impose rigid lines of demarcation between groups, particularly with respect to homosexual and heterosexual relations. True, it is often assumed that all transvestites are gay (the inaccuracy of this assumption is expanded in the following two chapters), but certainly many transvestites can be defined as exclusively heterosexual. Allen (1969) argues that the root of transvestism is in fact homosexuality and that the heterosexual transvestite is only apparently so; thus, those who do not display homosexual desires or sexual activities are designated repressed homosexuals. He finds that transvestites like to 'indulge' in alcohol, a similarity with homosexuals, because this permits both to express their repressed tendencies. Such diagnosis stands alone; while notions of repressed homosexuality have been mooted before, the idea that *all* transvestites are, at root, homosexual (and apparently alcohol dependent) receives no support in the literature.

This situation becomes complicated further if we consider the pre-operative transsexual (i.e. biologically male but considers himself female) who sees his relations with men as heterosexual and relations with women as lesbian, because he is 'really' female. The gay male partner of a male cross-dresser will be known as a 'straight gay' because he does not cross-dress, but when the other person adopts a female persona is s/he relating to the partner heterosexually or homosexually? If we take sexual interaction to be something more than what kind of genitals are put where, then the variations become necessarily diverse and confusing, but they underline two significant points: first, that attention to self-definition is often crucial if we are to comprehend the phenomenon of transvestism; second, that the conceptual boxes, so frequently imposed with the purpose of identifying clinical types, really do not have much explanatory value. Perhaps it would be more useful to think of these as overlapping categories in terms of the individual's own definition of his sexual orientation based on his gender identity at one moment in time. Thus the man who sees himself as homosexual in his relations with men, when he's a man with a masculine image, may in fact (and this is not always the case) see himself as relating heterosexually to men when he adopts a feminine appearance. Alternatively he may simply see himself as bisexual. While this goes some way towards clarifying part of the confusion generated in the socio-sexual interaction of biological males/social females with biological and social males, it does not shed much light on the heterosexual transvestite who wants to have sex with his wife while cross-dressed. He will regard this as heterosexuality but his wife may complain that this resembles lesbian sexuality (see Chapter 6). The clearest conclusion we can derive from this discussion is that the hard-and-fast concepts of masculine/feminine, straight/gay tend to fly out of the window in the context of cross-dressing and sexual orientation.

Why does a transvestite use feminine clothes? If it were simply a case of tactile sexual arousal linked with an object of clothing he would not need to wear it – arousal would be facilitated by feeling the object. Certainly transvestism goes beyond fetishism and incorporates gender and sexual needs. Langevin (1985) points out that cross-dressing is a label incorporating many meanings: it can be socially acceptable entertainment, it can be psychotic, violent, narcissistic, sado-masochistic, or none of these. Thus cross-dressing and transvestism are not one and the same thing – transvestism is one form of cross-dressing.

Transvestism tends to be very much a private activity, occurring behind closed doors, often a closely guarded secret admitted to very few others or no one at all. Consequently its incidence remains unknown, with medical practitioners and law enforcement agencies regarding it as a rare phenomenon. In 1928 the sexologist Havelock Ellis argued that transvestism was common, comparable in its incidence to homosexuality; more recently Randell (1975) has estimated that there may be 30 000 transvestites in Britain. Taking a more conservative attitude, Buckner (1970) has claimed that transvestism is restricted to a small minority, but this is based on his rather dubious notion that the demands placed upon the masculine role are steadily weakening. The only real certainty is the fact that, as a rule, transvestites do not come to medical or psychiatric attention unless they are suffering from some severe disturbance or are under pressure from either families or legal authorities. The effect of this has been to exacerbate the confusion characterising much of the medical and psychiatric literature where the case studies may well be atypical of transvestites in general.

Transvestism is not, and never has been, restricted to western culture, its universal character frequently attested to by reference to historical and cross-cultural material. Transvestism was found in ancient Greece, among the Roman emperors (notably Nero), the friends of Samuel Pepys and the French aristocracy of the eighteenth century. However, it has not always been seen in the same light and it has been suggested that possibly it was the Age of Reason which influenced a new direction in attitudes towards cross-dressing. The view emerged that such behaviour was irrational and a vice deserving of punishment; undoubtedly the extreme and outrageous deviations of the Victorian era can be considered as both reflections of, and reactions to, stringent moral repression.[4]

Looking at transvestism world-wide we find that it often becomes an integral part of magical and religious rituals, to the extent that a study of 76 non-western societies yielded evidence of socially acceptable cross-dressing in 49 of these cultures.[5] But to take cross-dressing as a unitary phenomenon is really fairly meaningless; it has to be located within a specific culture if we are to understand its dynamics and social ramifications. It has been used in fertility, marriage and funeral rites, as disguise to escape or avoid capture by the enemy, and as theatrical convention. And so, rather than being the case that some cultures are more accepting of cross-dressing than others, it is simply that the meanings attributed to it change and vary over time and from culture to culture. Indeed, even within one culture what is considered normal in one context may be deviant in another, hence the significance of ritual. In short, the jetstream over history and culture which is so commonly featured in much transvestite literature really tells us very little and we will remain none the wiser unless we attempt to understand the role that this phenomenon plays within a specific context, bound as it will be by historically and culturally shaped beliefs, attitudes and rules.

Where does this leave us in the attempt to identify the transvestite? Despite the range of variations it is, nevertheless, possible to list certain core characteristics which, when taken together, provide a realistic and workable description. First, the transvestite is a biological male who dresses periodically in feminine clothing with the intention of looking like a woman. Second, there is no necessary identification with a particular direction in sexual orientation; he is likely to be heterosexual but may be homosexual, possibly bisexual.[6] Third, he may derive sexual pleasure from dressing in women's clothing. His cross-dressing may be utterly private, an activity indulged in behind locked doors and known only to him. Alternatively, he may enjoy forays into the public world, deriving real satisfaction from being regarded and treated as a woman. But, unlike the transsexual, he wishes to remain biologically male and will not desire sex reassignment surgery.

But why should a man wish to appear as a member of the other, subordinate sex? And why should he derive pleasure, sexual or otherwise, from this dissemblance? Moreover, why should transvestism be such a one-way process? What is contained in the shaping and manifestation of gender and gender appearance that makes a man don the trappings and guise of femininity? Indeed, what is his image of femininity and to what extent does this tally with the realities of life as experienced by biological females? It is questions such as these which have been raised in a wealth of medical and psychiatric papers; however, the answers to such questions are less forthcoming. Certainly it appears that the issues surrounding gender and gender identity may provide us with the key to understanding what is, to all intents and purposes, a largely unknown and misunderstood form of behaviour. But before going on to unravel this web of claims and counter-claims, hypotheses and theories, it will be more profitable first to consider the transvestites themselves and the ways in which they view their lives. What we do know is that transvestism shocks a lot of people. The idea of a man dressing up as a woman for his own pleasure and not for entertainment evokes a range of reactions, none of them neutral. In western society our ideas of sex and gender are fixed; we hang on to them like an anchor in a rapidly changing and often confusing world. When a man enjoys dressing up in slinky underwear, high heels, make-up and a wig he is generally seen as 'weird' or 'perverted'. There is something wrong with him; he is deviant.

Finding transvestism

When a form of behaviour is widely considered to be deviant its investigation raises two problems: first, physical entry – securing admission to the relevant institution or meeting-place, whether it is a club of some sort, a mental hospital or a prison; second, social entry – gaining acceptance through winning the trust and confidence

of those under scrutiny. For this study the meeting-place was TV/TS
– the Transvestite/Transsexual Support Group – and entry was
surprisingly simple, established by one phone call to Yvonne, the
organiser. During my initial visit, Yvonne perched on the bar and,
calling for quiet, announced, 'This is Annie over here. She's a
psychiatrist and she's going to analyse all you freaks!' I doubt that
many sociologists have experienced such a rousing introduction to
their research subjects! People were interested, and throughout the
evening drifted over in ones and twos to ask me what I was doing. It
was clear that if Yvonne had given her approval, that was how things
would be. TV/TS has received several visitors in a research capacity
but, as they rarely attended more than once or twice, most people
were singularly unimpressed.

Subsequently I met people who were unaware of my research role
and assumed that I was the wife or friend of a transvestite. I decided
always to ensure that a person was aware of my interest before they
started to divulge personal information. Underlying this is a
commitment to honesty in research – people have a right to know
that they are being studied and, furthermore, the researcher must
demonstrate respect for her or his human subjects. The book itself
became a standing joke among the regulars in the group, and on
arrival I was usually greeted with, 'Hello Annie. Where's this
bleedin' book you're writing then?'

In this context being a woman had both advantages and
difficulties. Many of the transvestites clearly enjoyed the comparatively rare opportunity to talk with a 'real' woman who was not
going to react in a judgmental or critical way. This was an advantage
because people were willing to talk and would actively seek me out.
As I became more familiar to them, their acceptance grew until I
was considered to be one of the 'regulars'. I had arrived as an
unknown newcomer and also a rarity, a 'real' woman. Six months
later I left as a regular member, treated by many as a friend and even
confidante. I was shown hospitality and kindness, introduced to
many people, told life stories, asked for advice about clothes and
make-up, and teased a great deal – especially when I wore trousers;
and sometimes I was propositioned – but more of this later.

The outsider entering the transvestite sub-culture for the first
time will be confronted with a world turned inside out, a sub-world
where everyday events and transactions lose their usual significance. Ordinary expectations dissolve. Like Alice, it is as if reality

has passed through the looking-glass. The accepted signs and symbols of 'normality' are distorted and rearranged so that nothing remains the same. Men become 'women', the familiar badges of masculinity are discarded and replaced with a manufactured semblance of femininity, sometimes crudely and to ill-effect, at other times so successfully that one is at a loss to know 'what' one is seeing.

In other words, in a situation like this a significant change of context occurs; we move from an everyday world where we assume – at least in terms of sex and gender – that people are what they appear to be, to another artificial, fantasy world. That is not to say that the transvestite world consists only of men who can create a convincing persona of femininity – many certainly cannot – but this is a world where the outlandish becomes the norm. In such a context, I was the oddity, the outsider, both as a researcher and also (and more importantly) as the only 'real woman' present on most occasions. This conferred on me the status of the unusual, the exception to the rule where the normal became abnormal and vice versa. An example of this arose during my fourth visit to TV/TS when I was still in the process of getting to know people and building up rapport and trust with them. A transvestite, whom I had not met before, asked me if I was transsexual. I was shaken to say the least, having always approached the subject of my own gender identity (as opposed to gender role behaviour) unquestioningly. But in such a setting this type of question was to be expected. After all, in this world *I* was the exception, and usually a minority group of one. This eventually became quite a joke in the group; some of the members enjoyed fooling newcomers about my sexual identity and would often tease me with comments like, 'My God, Annie, you'll *never* pass if you carry on wearing trousers like that!'

Researching transvestism means entering a fantasy world where reality sometimes becomes a poor second to wishful thinking. Whether the situation is a club, a bar or a drag ball the thread running through and linking them together is that of dissembling – people pretending, both to themselves and others, that they are something other than what they really are. The effect of this is that it can be difficult to make sense of a situation, such as when a transvestite refers to her male self in the third person, or being told something only to discover later that this is pure fantasy or a lie. This presents difficulties for the researcher in two respects – firstly in terms of assessing the validity of information, and secondly in trying to ascertain accuracy without entering into too much gossip about individuals. What follows here is a study of transvestites based around a particular location, TV/TS. To claim that the members of TV/TS are representative of all transvestites would be foolhardy when we know nothing of the extent of transvestism, let alone the nature of all its practitioners. TV/TS provides a rare meeting-place for those who choose to go out and say, if only to like-minded people, 'I am a transvestite'.

TV/TS

TV/TS is based in London although it has a membership throughout the country. At the time of my research, meetings were held on weekend evenings in a large house in north London run by London Friend, a gay counselling organisation. TV/TS paid rent for its use of the building, raising this by charging a yearly membership subscription, a meeting attendance fee and also by organising raffles and social outings. The struggle to remain financially solvent was, and still is, constant, and is mainly undertaken by Yvonne Sinclair, a transvestite, who is the organiser, along with other volunteers. Besides providing a social meeting-point for transvestites and transsexuals and their partners, the group also runs a telephone helpline, and contact with the national membership is maintained through the monthly magazine, *Glad Rag*.

Glad Rag was initiated at the end of 1982 following a decision to change the group into a club with formal membership and a yearly subscription. The plan was to expand membership by means of the monthly magazine and thereby increase the group's funding with a view to saving sufficient money to obtain permanent premises. At first *Glad Rag* was published in photocopy format. Six months later it changed to booklet form. However, there was little concrete information contained in the magazine and much of the space was taken up with in-group (and out-group) bickering. The format changed again with the appointment of a new editor and the setting-up of an editorial group. By the beginning of 1987 each issue had a print run of 1000 copies. Today the magazine consists of an editorial, newspaper reports of special interest to members, letters and stories. The stories focus on issues directly relevant to the cross-dresser: passing (being taken for a woman in public), famous transvestite figures in history, and some satire, such as 'Jasmine Bond – Very Special Agent 00274', a send-up of the Beaumont Society (an organisation which caters specifically to heterosexual transvestites), written in the style of a James Bond novel.

Attendance at meetings fluctuated considerably, with a central core of regulars and a large periphery of others. Meetings tended to be less well attended in the summer when daylight-saving time removes the protective cover of darkness. The building was vulnerable to attack and had been highlighted in a fascist publication because it is a meeting-place for gay and lesbian groups, so the glass door was protected by a steel mesh screen and operated by entry phone, necessary for security but unwelcoming all the same. The meeting-room had a counter, tables and chairs, set out like a coffee-bar. At the back there was a room for those who preferred to change on arrival. The helpline phone, housed in a quiet room at the top of the house, was connected to an extra earpiece so that others being trained to give advice and counselling could listen to calls. The overall impression of the place was one of drabness, starved as it was of the financial support necessary for a greater degree of comfort and cheerful surroundings. The heating was supplied by means of a portable gas-fire and so in winter the rooms were often chilly.

In 1986 the group moved to new premises in the East End of London. Originally an old factory, the building was in an appalling state of repair and in need of total transformation. At the time of writing the rehabilitation process is moving towards completion, with a large meeting area, a kitchen upstairs, and changing rooms, an office and a further meeting space on the ground floor. The total overheads, including rental, are estimated to run between £26 000 and £30 000 a year. This amount comes from subscriptions and voluntary donations as the group does not receive any form of public funding. The building provides a more welcoming and comfortable venue and, as a result, is attracting a growing membership. At present this stands at approximately 1000. A new venture is the Partners' Support Group which is discussed further in Chapter 5.

A typical evening at TV/TS involved about twenty people, not all of them cross-dressed. Usually there were no 'real' women present, although occasionally a transvestite was accompanied by his wife.

(There are now more wives attending, largely as a result of the Partners' Support Group.) For the newcomer, the outstanding feature of the meetings is, of course, appearance. Visually TV/TS represents a very mixed bag with respect to dress styles, make-up skills, attention to detail and so on. Most transvestites tend to prefer more stereotypically 'feminine' types of clothes, such as high-heeled shoes, tight skirts or dresses, but there was a good deal of variation. Some of the transvestites may well have succeeded in passing as women in the public world, but others looked like men trying to dress as women with none of the panache and style associated with, say, the drag artist. Cheap wigs, often in an overly youthful style or inappropriate colour, false eyelashes and heavy panstick make-up were obvious factors, but other telltale signs such as beard shadow, hairy arms, sometimes complete with tattoos, bushy eyebrows, large hands and prominent adam's apples were all indicative of male sex. Prior to my first visit to TV/TS I was warned to expect some odd sights and certainly this proved to be the case. A person, obviously male, in an ill-fitting mini dress, synthetic wig and heavy make-up which failed to camouflage beard shadow would provoke ridicule and censure in other circumstances, but at TV/TS all attempts at cross-dressing were more or less accepted, with some good-natured teasing from time to time. Variations in appearance were accepted on the basis that some had not, as yet, developed the necessary degree of skill required to contrive a convincing image of femininity, or that they often did not possess the means to finance two wardrobes. Even if money was less of a problem there still remained the hurdle of going out and buying women's clothes.

A convincing gender persona clearly extends beyond the superficial features of dress and make-up. These aspects make for the initial impact, but this can quickly become transparent when other components of gender appearance are missing. Body movements, gestures and facial expressions are all part of the learned process of the outward manifestations of gender role. Consequently a feminine appearance was often contradicted by identifiably masculine body movements, such as the gestures and facial expressions involved in lighting a cigarette, or the eye movements in face-to-face conversation. It is this area which probably presents the greatest difficulty for many transvestites, because such attributes, while learned, are performed unconsciously by the time the person is an adult. Thus the process of unlearning a lifetime's habits, and then learning new ones to be adopted on a temporary basis only, calls for hard work, concentration and a sharp eye for detail. At times I was aware of being watched closely. I would sometimes even be asked to demonstrate a simple movement, such as getting up from a chair. Obviously I have no monopoly on feminine movements, but the point here is that I was behaving and moving in an automatic fashion, based on years of habit, and not attempting to be something quite different. The obvious emphasis on appearance made me conscious at first of my own dress. I began to wonder what I should wear to fit in. I decided that it would be easier for me to dress as I normally would – trousers and sweaters – for my own comfort, and also as this helped to convey to others that I was 'real'. This decision was later reaffirmed at drag balls, where I could never meet the extravagant and outrageous standards of dress adopted.

Most of the transvestites would arrive already cross-dressed, but some, either because they were married or because they feared travelling on public transport, would change during the evening, although not all would do so. This change of appearance and identity caused me some confusion when, for example, a man would arrive, bag in hand, and be greeted as 'Jim', disappear into the back room and emerge some time later as 'Julie'. There were even a few times when I did not connect the male and the 'female' as one and the same person.

After my first visit I began to think about the way I saw cross-dressed men. Did I treat them as men, or as women, or as men-appearing-as-women? This was highlighted by an incident which occurred during my third visit to TV/TS. While chatting with a transvestite I had met previously, I noticed someone standing at the counter. She looked different from the others present, dressed in a quiet manner with light make-up and glasses. Her own hair was done in an ordinary, unelaborate style. Unremarkable in appearance, she could have been a secretary or receptionist. Not having met her before, I wanted to introduce myself and, hopefully, find out more about her. But I found myself unable to approach her until I knew 'what' she was. In other words, I realised that my social manner towards her would be determined by my knowledge of her sexual status. The everyday, taken-for-granted assumption that gender appearance indicates biological sex broke down in this setting and thus the fragility of that commonplace expectation was thrown into sharp relief. She could have been a transvestite or, indeed, she could have been a real woman. *I* was unable to tell. The very fact that I had to ascertain her biological status from someone else before approaching her underlined the ways in which social interaction is firmly based on the unconscious expectations we use to identify people and place them in stereotyped categories.

With few exceptions I treated cross-dressed men as precisely that. I could not perceive them as women, no matter how convincing their appearance, gestures and voice might be, because I already knew that they were *not* women. However, they did not appear to be men either. It was almost as though I developed a third conceptual category in order to interact with them. More often than not a convincing feminine appearance would be contradicted by an unmistakably male voice, but this had a less disorientating effect than might be expected initially because this applied to most people at TV/TS. Thus it became the norm. Additionally, it would seem that when visual perception is contradicted by the aural, the visual predominates. It was, therefore, less disconcerting than would be supposed, with the exception of telephone conversations where the visual is absent. Invariably, I could not identify voices, even those I came to know well. Some transsexuals were receiving voice therapy but others lightened their tone of voice by speaking very quietly. This tended to inhibit conversation in noisy surroundings.

The other people attending TV/TS fell into two groups: the partners of transvestites and transsexuals, and the punters. Now and then the wife of a transvestite attended, but usually the partners were homosexual men who did not cross-dress. The gay couples presented some fascinating illustrations of gender role-playing and variations on roles. Most of them acted very much as couples – i.e. as if they were married – yet not all the cross-dressing partners lived full-time as women. Some were employed in typically masculine occupations. When dressed, however, they behaved in overtly feminine ways, holding on to their partner's arm, turning to him for approval and sitting on his knee.

A particularly striking example of such role-playing emerged at the TV/TS Christmas party. Tony, the male partner of Jenny, a transvestite who worked in the day as a man, arrived at the party cross-dressed. He explained that Jenny was angry with him because he had wanted to come to the party dressed up, as it was a special occasion. She had refused to come with him, in much the same way as the wife of a heterosexual transvestite might refuse to accompany her husband when he was cross-dressed. A week later I had supper with a group of transvestites at Tony's and Jenny's flat, prior to going to a drag ball with them. Jenny was sitting in masculine work-clothes, sulking and refusing to speak to anyone. It transpired that Tony was planning to go to the ball in drag and Jenny was again refusing to go. On the way to the ball Tony explained that Jenny hated him dressing up and would not be seen with him when he did. He stressed to me that he was not a transvestite and that he only liked to dress up for special events; in fact he referred to it as 'going out in drag', and not as 'dressing', which is the terminology of transvestism. In a wig, high-heeled shoes, and a dress he had made out of kitchen curtains, Tony remained Tony, changing neither his name nor his behaviour, unlike a transvestite. At another ball a few days later he appeared resplendent in a three-piece suit with a smiling Jenny on his arm; although disappointed at not being able to wear an evening gown and compete with the extravagant styles on display, he had compromised in order to keep the peace.

Each meeting of TV/TS was attended by a small number of mainly middle-aged and apparently working-class men. They always acknowledged me courteously but, unlike the others, made no attempt to engage me in conversation beyond the usual pleasantries about the weather. Yvonne informed me that these men were punters, who either cannot or will not admit to their own homosexuality, describing them as men 'who don't want to go to bed with a man, but don't want to go to bed with a real woman either'. From time to time one of them would disappear upstairs with a transvestite to one of the empty rooms. On seeing me notice a couple slip out one evening, Yvonne remarked, 'There goes someone for a flash of french knickers!'. Although such activities were regarded as normal and unremarkable by those present, there was virtually no display of physical affection in the main room itself, apart from kisses proffered in greeting.

Meetings comprised an all-white group which spanned the class spectrum from manual workers to professionals. People were there because they were involved, directly or indirectly, with transvestism. It was this factor alone which operated as a common bond. There were groups of friends who met more frequently, but many came alone, often because they were married. Small groups congregated around the tables, and a few sat at the counter chatting to Yvonne, who always presided over the gathering. Typically the evening would be spent in light-hearted conversation. As these were unstructured social gatherings it was difficult to ask too many personal questions in a group situation. It was easier to get a great deal more information in one-to-one conversations and I usually made a point of spending time with one person during each visit. Thus I was able to build up a picture of individual lives, with opinions and views on ways of coping with transvestism.

Unlike the social circle of, for instance, the local pub or wine-bar, people tended not to discuss the week's events at home or work. For the majority of them, this related to their masculine lives and, for that evening at least, they had become another person. This meant that it was not easy to pick up details about jobs and lifestyles without direct questions. Anecdotes related to cross-dressing sprinkled the conversation. Several transvestites recounted, with obvious pleasure, instances of shopping, eating in a restaurant or going to the cinema cross-dressed and 'passing', not being 'read' or caught out. More commonly though, the story would run along the lines of all going well until they were read by a group of young children who subsequently turned their attention to the victim, shouting out that he was really a man. The transvestite will often avoid children because they tend to be less taken in by the contrived semblance of femininity than adults. Stories involving the police always resulted in great hilarity, such as being stopped for speeding and trying to nod and smile speechlessly so as not to be given away by a deep male voice, simultaneously praying that the police officer would not ask to see their driving licence.

Weekend clubbing

TV/TS usually closed between 11 p.m. and midnight, and after washing-up and tidying the room there would usually be some discussion about where to go next, whether to go to this club or that bar, and although always invited, I only went when accompanied by Yvonne, for reasons to be explained later. Usually we visited a club in an hotel catering to gay men. The bar was crowded, hot and smoky, with a disco and a tiny dance floor. Upstairs there was a restaurant, television room and sitting room, all pleasantly and tastefully decorated. The bar stayed open, illegally, until 3 a.m., and although formal membership was not required, entry was vetted by a male receptionist who insisted that a guest-book be signed, even if only with fictitious names. As Yvonne was well known, entry was guaranteed. The bar and the rest of the hotel were frequented by gay men. Transvestites and transsexuals were allowed in on Friday and Saturday nights. There was some hostility on the part of gay men towards the cross-dressed men, although there were also several drag artists in full drag, who entertained at clubs and pubs. The drag artists presented a feminine persona in the most dramatic manner. One in particular, an ex-marine, 6 feet 6 inches tall in stilettos, swathed in feather boas and extraordinarily long false eyelashes could, I was told, 'blow the lid off the government' if she ever chose to write her memoirs.

I had the impression that I was the only biological woman at the club but, of course, it was difficult to be absolutely certain without questioning people directly. Despite not liking the place very much, there were two distinct advantages to be gained from visiting fairly often. First, the drinking and dancing provided a more relaxed social setting and, especially in the early stages, this eased my transition from newcomer to regular member of the group. Second, and more important, it provided opportunities to talk at greater length with individuals with less chance of being overheard or interrupted than at TV/TS. In this way I was able to gather a great deal more information about people's life histories, their lives at present and their attitudes towards transvestism and associated topics.

However, this was also a territory where, unlike TV/TS, my identity as a researcher was not generally known and, from the questions put to Yvonne or directly to me, it was clear that some wondered what a woman was doing at the club. Sometimes it was assumed that my sexual preference was for cross-dressed men and I was occasionally propositioned along these lines. But I was never entirely sure if the propositions were based on my real sex or the assumption that I was a man passing as a woman. This would put me in the position of thinking: 'Is s/he transvestite or transsexual? Does s/he think I'm transvestite, transsexual or a woman? Is s/he relating to me male to male, female to female, male to female, or female to male?' Not only was I seen as 'fair game' by some, but it was also a matter of debate as to 'what' I was at times. When a woman is approached by a man there are certain cues and strategies – visual and verbal – that she has learned to employ in appropriate situations, resorting if necessary to hostility if she does not want his attention. However, in the club I had to negotiate a fairly tricky route of not being directly rude to people whose goodwill I needed to cultivate, while also considering my own safety. In a situation like this, simple matters such as visiting the toilet become problematic, given that 'Ladies' was taken to refer to gender appearance only and not to biological sex! This may sound rather prissy, but the point here is that many of the people who visited the club did so with the express purpose of picking someone up. Thus avoidance of the less public areas was advisable, especially given the assumptions made about my reasons for being there. This problem was solved by Yvonne, who insisted on accompanying me, clearing everyone out of the toilets, waiting outside and refusing to allow anyone in, and then returning me to our group! She always kept a very close eye on me and it was this protective attitude which made it possible for me to go to the club and stay there till the early hours. Throughout the research period Yvonne acted as my 'minder' and in doing so minimised some of the harassment that I encountered. The irony here is that I had to rely on a man (dressed as a woman) to protect me from other men (also dressed as women) – an interesting variation on the more usual state of affairs.

This, then, is how I viewed the 'looking-glass world' of those transvestites whose cross-dressing extends beyond the privacy of the bedroom and bathroom into the semi-public world of TV/TS and specialised leisure facilities. For some, their social life revolves around transvestism, going to TV/TS, clubs and bars every weekend. For others, especially those who are married, this is a more occasional leisure pursuit which has to be balanced against the other demands of family life and may well be supplemented by cross-dressing at home. Some transvestites spend most of their time cross-dressed, while others engage in the activity much less frequently, although a common complaint from wives is that their husbands 'dress' too often at home. Others who live in small towns may only be able to involve themselves in this social world every few weeks or months, depending on their ability, financial and otherwise, to spend a weekend in London.

   I saw the scene as a stranger and an outsider. My impressions were unavoidably influenced both by being a non-participant in cross-dressing and by the fact that I was usually the only biological woman present. Although at times I felt uncomfortable and occasionally had to deal with awkward situations, the fact of being female was also an advantage. It afforded a degree of rapport and enthusiasm from the transvestites which probably would not have been shown to a non-transvestite male researcher. For example, the transvestites were keen to talk to me – asking advice about clothes and make-up and telling me about the problems they were having with their wives. It is unlikely that they would have reacted to a man in the same way, especially in terms of social chit-chat, which was an important ice-breaker and way of moving on to more personal topics. Having set the scene, so to speak, from the standpoint of the observer, we can now turn to the principle actors, the transvestites themselves.

3

Best of both worlds? Transvestite lives

> 'In some ways I'm thankful I'm a TV because my life would be very boring otherwise. It's nice to be somebody different, it means I can look at life from two different levels.'
>
> (Elaine)

Case studies are quite common in the professional literature dealing with transvestism and transsexualism whereby individuals receiving medical or psychiatric treatment are utilised to illustrate more theoretically directed accounts.[1] In many instances, however, the reader is not left with any mental picture of the individuals under scrutiny but instead is presented with a list of characteristics which have often been predefined as revelant to the root causes of their behaviour. A comparison of various aspects of the literature results in an amalgam of contradictory factors. The result is that we are left with little information concerning the transvestite as an individual.

The purpose of this chapter is to provide some 'portraits' of transvestites. The term 'portraits' is used rather than the more usual 'case studies', because they have not been drawn up in accordance with a predetermined check-list of factors, as in some medico-psychiatric studies. Rather they are images developed over time, derived from lengthy conversations, from snippets of information which were subsequently followed up, and repeated observation. In this respect these portraits do not adhere to any quantitative methodology claiming perfect detachment and objectivity. Certainly a questionnaire provides a more standardised approach; it can be examined in terms of what questions were asked and so on; but it excludes the dynamics and the feel of real events. This is particularly pertinent when referring to situations of which most people have no direct experience. Research carried out through participant observation is a kind of reportage; and such reporting can only be mediated through the researcher's own perceptual capacities. Alternative views could be offered, and it is, of course, an easy matter to criticise such portraits for lack of authenticity. They can at best be no more than partial. Some offer biographical details, others provide glimpses into specific aspects of a life, all belong to a particular point in time. Together they provide insights into a way of life unknown to the majority of people.

Fieldwork at TV/TS and at social venues offered contact with a large number of transvestites. Whereas in more mundane circumstances an individual will be unlikely to divulge much in the way of personal information on the strength of a few meetings with someone, the very fact of attending TV/TS tended to have the effect of disclosure. Although for many their cross-dressing may have previously occurred only in private, their presence at TV/TS served to propel them into some sort of public outspokenness, allowing them to divulge a heretofore hidden secret to a group of like-minded people. This meant that it was possible, right from the start, to ask direct, personal questions about transvestism and the effect that it had on their lives.

The individuals featured below have been selected on two counts: as examples of variations in cross-dressing, such as the older transvestite, or the 'full-time woman'; and as examples of individuals who, in varying ways, played a central part during fieldwork. In some cases the dividing line between transvestism and transsexualism becomes blurred. How do we categorise the person who has periodically cross-dressed throughout his life and then decides, in his sixties, to have sex reassignment surgery? And when the outcome is not a happy one the problem of finding the appropriate label broadens. Was that person 'really' a transsexual all along, or a transvestite who, by recourse to private medicine, took one step too many? In all the portraits given here and in subsequent chapters individual transvestites are referred to in the gender in which they usually appeared; that is to say, 'he' becomes 'she'; transvestites in general are referred to as 'he'.

The younger transvestite

The younger transvestite may spend the week working as a man, using his leisure time for cross-dressing. This sort of lifestyle renders the development of feminine features through hormone therapy, electrolysis and depilation much more of a problem. While beard growth or bushy eyebrows will counteract a contrived feminine appearance, this is less crucial at TV/TS or a specialist leisure venue. In contrast to this, plucked eyebrows, traces of make-up or nail varnish can act as dangerous betrayals contradicting both physical and social masculinity. The development of breasts through oestrogen use presents even greater difficulties. In short, the transvestite who attempts to live as a male in public and a female in private is, in fact, living a double life and necessarily experiences the stresses and strains associated with such a lifestyle. The reverse of these problems is that the younger transvestite will have grown up during a period when attitudes towards sexuality began to relax in some respects. So while older individuals had to cope with the narrower, more restrictive morality of the 1940s and 1950s, the younger transvestite reached adolescence at a time when, with the legacy of the 1960s' philosophy of hedonism and 'doing your own thing', those strictures were losing their traditional hold.

Elaine

At twenty-eight Elaine is self-confident and conveys a sense of ease with herself. She visited TV/TS and clubs regularly and we had many long conversations about her transvestism, her past, and her current lifestyle. Like many transvestites, Elaine's childhood and early teenage years were fraught with conflict and the fear of discovery, but London in the early 1970s provided an escape into a world not only of sex, drugs and rock 'n roll but, more importantly, tolerance. Thus she had the opportunity to live out previously unfulfilled fantasies.

Although Elaine remembers thinking about wearing female clothing from the age of five, she did not actually attempt to do so until she was fourteen. She describes her childhood as ordinary and unremarkable; a late starter at school, she eventually caught up and left school at sixteen with some qualifications. Although aware of being different, Elaine insists that she did not feel guilty about her desire to wear female clothing. Nevertheless, she was careful not to give any clues to her school friends.

Elaine's life changed dramatically at thirteen when her mother died of cancer. As an only child, she was expected to 'take over the female gender role', to do the cooking and cleaning during the week as her father worked long hours. It was at this time that she began cross-dressing, making use of the two hours alone at home before her father returned from work. She bought her first make-up while on holiday at a seaside resort, telling the shop assistant that it was a present for her sister. Then she bought a wig, this time presenting the hairdresser with a note supposedly written by the same, fictitious, sister.

Fantasy fulfilment was further enhanced by the perks attached to a weekend gardening job for a local, wealthy family. Discarded clothing, intended for use as rags, could be retrieved and added to Elaine's wardrobe. Also, when the family was out, she would take clothes from the washing line, masturbate, and then carefully return them. As there were several teenage girls in the family Elaine could occasionally steal items which were not missed.

After a year or so Elaine had amassed a fair amount of clothing, underwear, make-up and wigs from various sources, all of which was hidden in a box under her bed. The inevitable happened when her father retrieved a newspaper which had slipped down between the wall and the bed: 'I thought I was going to die.' Stunned, her father asked her to get rid of it. Although she was very upset about it, Elaine did so, feeling that she had no choice but to comply with her father's request. She had to be content with her fantasies until a year later when her father remarried and Elaine found that her stepmother's clothes fitted her. Her stepmother had no idea that her clothes were being used in this way, and Elaine suspects that her father put the issue out of his mind, preferring not to think about it and hoping that his remarriage had established greater security and stability in his son's life.

Elaine started on forays into the outside world, walking round

Epping Forest at night, hoping not to be seen, 'because I wasn't
good enough to be convincing', but deriving a thrill from the fear of
discovery. By this time she had started dating girls and had become
heterosexually active. Her father moved to another county, but
Elaine remained behind to complete an accountancy course at the
local technical college. The transition from private, secret
cross-dressing to coming out occurred when Elaine found a
two-page article in a guide to 'alternative' London about a
transvestite commune in south London. She contacted Release, an
advice agency, obtained the phone number and from then on visited
the commune every weekend. Here she began a sexual relationship
with Moira, a post-operative transsexual. She also embarked on her
first homosexual experiences by placing an advert in *Time Out* (a
weekly 'what's on' magazine), 'because I wanted to experience men,
to see what it was like'. A male accounts clerk during the week,
Elaine would be 'a girl for the weekend', go out cross-dressed to
clubs with other transvestites, flirt with men and tell them that she
was a post-operative transsexual. 'Those were the halcyon days. I
was a bright young thing on the scene.'

By the early 1970s the clubs had started to close down and the
scene was no longer as exciting as it had been. Elaine transferred to
a job in the City and found a steady girlfriend. Considering
marriage, she thus decided to confess her transvestism. Her
girlfriend was not overjoyed at the revelation, and so Elaine
suggested that she and a close friend Alan, in whom she had already
confided, come to a club so that they might see her dressed. As a
result, the girlfriend broke off the relationship and became engaged
to Alan!

Elaine insists that she is truly bisexual, although she prefers sex
with women: 'I like girls so much I want to be one.' She would love
to have a steady girlfriend but finds that women are not prepared to
tolerate her transvestism. Consequently relationships have always
tended to crumble when faced with such confessions. Most of
Elaine's sexual relationships are now with men, but she likes to
come to TV/TS as a man because 'I get turned on by femininity and I
like to pick them up'. She lives alone and spends most weekends at
clubs or at TV/TS where she helps to organise the group and to run
the helpline. I asked her how she saw herself in ten years' time. She
laughed and replied, 'Dead! I live for today and never think about
it. Dead from AIDS probably!'

The older transvestite

The onset of middle age is associated with both advantages and difficulties for the transvestite. On the one hand, voice pitch becomes less of a problem, as the older woman's voice often deepens and thus the disparity between female appearance and male voice becomes less noticeable. In contrast, middle age can be accompanied by hair loss and baldness. When this occurs the transvestite is no longer able to style his own hair and reliance on wigs becomes essential. The progression to baldness can be arrested to some extent by hormone treatment, but this cannot replace hair that has already been lost and the effects continue only if the hormones are taken on a regular basis. The decision to live full-time as a woman makes hormone therapy a more practical option, as the problems of concealing a feminised anatomy while in the male role no longer arise. In some respects, middle age can provide certain advantages for the transvestite which are not always available to his younger counterpart.

Lucy

In her sixties, Lucy looks and acts the part of an older woman convincingly, dressed and made-up appropriately for her age. As her voice has the deeper pitch associated more with this age group, it complements rather than contradicts her general appearance. In many respects Lucy's story represents a typical aspect of the lifestyle of the older transvestite. She married in 1940, telling her wife about her transvestism prior to the wedding, 'But we were both very young and I don't think either of us knew what it was.' After marriage Lucy tried hard not to cross-dress, relying on the one respite which occurred each summer when her wife visited her own family, taking their daughter with her. During this time Lucy would take the opportunity to cross-dress continually, deriving great satisfaction from her annual 'binge'. She did not hide this from her wife and thus it was accepted that their respective vacations would be spent in this way.

In 1954 Lucy became increasingly depressed, experiencing the world as a monotone of grey, as lifeless and worthless. Eventually her wife responded by saying to Lucy, 'Look, if you feel like that about it you'd better get on with it'; but she added one proviso – that the neighbours were not to know. After that, Lucy began to dress more frequently, not only during her wife's yearly absence, but also in her presence. This worked out fairly well and caused remarkably little friction between them, even to the extent that when Lucy asked her wife years later if she minded, the response was that she did not really notice it any longer.

Lucy's wife died in 1978. After this Lucy began to cross-dress more frequently. While chatting on the telephone one day a neighbour, Alice, came into the house without knocking and discovered Lucy. 'I'm dressed as a woman,' said Lucy, to which Alice replied, 'Yes, I can see that.' Lucy asked her if she might prefer to walk out of the house again, but Alice said she was not bothered and that her suspicions had already been roused on seeing Lucy's rather large court-shoes in the wardrobe. Since then Lucy and Alice, who is also alone, have spent several holidays together with Lucy always dressed as a woman.

Lucy argues that transvestism is an obsession which cannot be relinquished. 'It's like drugs,' she says, and as the time passes so the addiction becomes stronger and more deeply entrenched. Although religious and active in the Spiritualist Church, Lucy does not perceive any conflict between her religious beliefs and her transvestite practices, a reflection perhaps of the less orthodox approach of this particular church.

Unlike some transvestites, Lucy's story is not one of continual mental torment and repeated attempts to suppress her transvestism, but rather it suggests a life of relatively easy compromise. However, we only have Lucy's side of the story. We cannot know how her wife really felt about it. Was she as tolerant and unruffled by her husband's cross-dressing as Lucy maintained? Impossible as this may be to ascertain, the views of transvestites' wives discussed in Chapter 6 should add a cautionary note.

Anne

Like Lucy, Anne also presents a picture of an older transvestite for whom lifestyle changes have brought about greater opportunities for cross-dressing. Although for Lucy this followed her wife's death, Anne made the decision to leave her family in order to live alone as a woman.

With short, demi-waved, brown hair of her own and glasses, Anne looks like a middle-aged, middle-class, suburban housewife. She likes to think of herself as fairly up to date and dresses accordingly. She attempts to deal with her height of almost six feet by wearing flat shoes and long dresses, thereby creating the appearance of a respectable and conventional person. We met on many occasions at TV/TS as well as drag balls. Because Anne was always open, friendly and willing to talk, she was an accessible subject.

Anne was atypical of the group, as she came from a more middle-class background, her father having made his career in the higher echelons of the armed forces. At the age of four Anne was sent to a convent school which took in a few boys. Around this time she was punished for some misdemeanour by being made to put on a dress and sit with the girls in the class – 'and I *hated* it!' she said. She says this stimulated an interest in female clothing however, and she took to trying on her sister's clothes and wearing them in bed at night. After infants' school, Anne was sent to a boys' school but often wished that she could have attended the girls' school instead.

Military training at Sandhurst was followed by several years in the army. Anne recalled that during that time she was aware of feeling different. Although she was unable to pinpoint the feeling, its direction or cause, she knew she was not like other men. In the barracks she hated undressing in front of them and felt embarrassed when she could not avoid it. She took up boxing, despite disliking sport intensely, a choice which she later considered to be over-compensation. She did not experience any homosexual leanings but when she and her colleagues visited brothels she would not have sexual intercourse, preferring instead to dress in the prostitute's clothes. Anne often stressed that she was a very good soldier, that she did her job well and was never cowardly. 'But then women aren't cowards, are they?'

On returning to London, Anne met a woman penfriend of some years. On the day after their first meeting they became engaged. 'It was a big mistake, I should never have married. I suppose I thought marriage would cure me.' The marriage resulted in five children, now all adults. Her wife always detested Anne's cross-dressing and so a pattern emerged which is common to many transvestites: periodic binges followed by a purge in which all the clothes are given away or destroyed.

Having established her own business as a sales representative supplying textile firms in southern England, Anne made the decision to live full-time as a woman, and had recently left her wife. She had just written to all her clients explaining the situation and expressing the hope that they would continue to do business with her. The response was far more positive than she had dared to hope. In fact, she recounted her first meetings with her clients when she appeared in her new gender with obvious gusto and enjoyment. One client, who had failed to recognise her, burst out laughing when she identified herself and said, 'Well, bugger me, you do spring some surprises, don't you!' Anne was clearly delighted by this and relished this first indication of acceptance by business colleagues.

While Anne's self-confidence and belief that she'd made a correct decision had been boosted by these encounters, she was also receiving the medical support of a major consultant in sex reassignment treatment. The physical effects of hormone therapy were becoming apparent and she was proud that she had developed breasts, that her hips had broadened and her waist had slimmed down. She had been approved for sex reassignment surgery but, unlike many who reach this stage, would be able to avoid lengthy delays by her ability to pay for her treatment at a private clinic. Anne perceived this as the final stage of becoming female; not for sexual reasons – insisting that 'at my age I don't have any sexual urges'; her only concern was to become female in body as well as in dress. This, however, was likely to be delayed because she was still married and thus had to obtain her wife's consent. As both were Roman Catholic, divorce would not be possible; additionally Anne's wife refused to have anything to do with the affair. Anne remained optimistic, however, sure that her wife would provide the necessary signature in a few months. Her children's attitudes were more ambivalent, but the youngest had accepted the situation and invited Anne to visit over the Christmas holiday.

At this time Anne gave a consistent impression of enthusiasm and enjoyment of life at all times, always bright and cheerful, seemingly well-balanced and happy with her new role. At drag balls she would spend the evening dancing or chatting with friends in a relaxed, unself-conscious manner, the epitome of the person who had found what she wanted in life. It was not possible to meet Anne's wife, but what story would she have offered? Nearly thirty years of marriage had been ended, not by her husband leaving her for another woman, but by her husband becoming another woman! What explanation did she give friends, family and neighbours? While Lucy's wife had tolerated the cross-dressing, she had insisted that the neighbours should not find out; one can only speculate on the degree of shame and stress experienced by Anne's wife.

Both Lucy and Anne presented an appearance suitable to middle age, with dress, hairstyle, make-up, voice and general manner appropriate to their middle years. However, not all transvestites are as realistic. Some tend to dress in a style more fitting for someone many years their junior. Sophie, plump, middle-aged and married, chose short skirts and heavy make-up but, aware of the inappropriateness of her dress, would laugh it off heartily, stressing that she only did it for fun. In direct contrast to Sophie stood Suzanne, probably in her sixties, in heavy panstick make-up, false eyelashes, obviously synthetic wig styled into a youthful bob, short skirt and long gloves to disguise masculine-looking hands. Although she claimed to be Austrian, she spoke with a heavy French accent, but she was apparently English. Self-conscious and shy, Suzanne represented the obverse of the Annes in the transvestite world. Sometimes she disappeared upstairs with one of the punters who visited TV/TS.

The reality of transvestites in their fifties and sixties (or even older) is not often found in popular imagery, possibly because ideals of feminine beauty are associated with youth and also because such behaviour is associated with sexual deviance and thus again with a younger age group. Yet both Lucy and Anne cross-dressed from a very young age and continued to do so periodically throughout their lives, appearing for the most part as ordinary men with wives and families.

Anne, on the other hand, exemplifies the difficulties encountered when attempting to divide transvestism and transsexualism into entirely separate categories. Having spent the greater part of her life thinking of herself as a transvestite and acting accordingly, she then, like a small number of transvestites, decided to live as a 'full-time woman'. Not content to remain as a biological male beneath the feminine guise and, no doubt, influenced by her financial resources, she made the decision to cross over by opting for reassignment surgery.

Anne was optimistic about her future, confident that the legal wrangles with her wife would be resolved, that she would eventually achieve her goal of becoming a female anatomically as well as socially. However, although she had had the operation and subsequently left London, her dreams of a new life as a woman were shattered, reality falling far short of her expectations. The wonderful feelings of euphoria which she had anticipated experiencing had not occurred. The special significance that Anne, as a man, had attached to the wearing of feminine clothing no longer applied, and pangs of regret were setting in, emphasised all the more by developing agoraphobia. Having thrown in her job she found work in a petrol station, only to be attacked by a gang of youths who thought she was a man in drag. Her attempt to accompany a much younger transvestite friend to a dance-hall met with a refusal to allow her entry on the grounds that she, not her girlfriend, was a man in drag. Anne discovered the hard way, as indeed many do, that it is not so easy to change one's sex/gender. Now she faces the rest of her life living in limbo, neither man nor woman.

The 'full-time woman'

While the transvestite and the transsexual may seem to represent little more than variations on the common theme of men dressing as women, they do, in fact, comprise different categories. The transvestite periodically cross-dresses with the intention of taking on the appearance of the opposite sex, whereas the transsexual actually wishes to become a woman, claiming to have been trapped in the wrong body. This distinction could often be readily identified at TV/TS. Some transvestites made little pretence of being anything other than a man dressed up as a woman; others extended the semblance and make considerable efforts to adopt ostensibly feminine gestures, mannerisms and body movements. It is in the case of the full-time transvestite who has not undergone sex reassignment surgery that the distinction becomes blurred, and although several members of TV/TS were hoping to be granted this surgery, the fact remains that they were still genitally male, even when hormone treatment enabled them to develop breasts.

Thus the question concerning the differences between the transvestite and the transsexual finds no easy answer, especially as the very fact of living as a full-time, or almost full-time, woman does not automatically entail a definition of self as transsexual. The few cases which have received extensive media coverage in Britain – April Ashley, Jan Morris and Julia Grant – are regarded predominantly as exceptions in the transsexual/transvestite world, and sometimes as oddities who were publicity hungry and traded privacy for financial gain.

It is within this grey area of the full-time transvestite that the outsider experiences confusion when confronting people who are outwardly female and yet biologically male. So convincing is the appearance of some that social detection of their real sex is almost impossible. At a drag ball I learned that the beautiful woman in the pierrot costume was in fact a full-time transvestite who, on receiving a prison sentence, had initially been sent to Holloway, a women's prison. In many respects the differences between the transvestite and the so-called transsexual lie with their own perceptions and definitions of self: whether they consider themselves 'real women' or whether they see cross-dressing as an end in itself which allows partial entry into the world of femininity. Such distinctions are exemplified by the following portraits: Margaret, a biological male who lives and works as a woman, defines herself as transsexual and claims to understand 'what it means to be a woman', and Yvonne, a transvestite who claims to be nothing more than 'a fella in a frock'.

Margaret

When I saw Margaret I thought that in any other circumstances the idea that she might not be a woman would never arise. Small in stature and slightly built, she had the advantage of not needing to camouflage height or bone structure. She was dressed in a denim two-piece suit, polo-neck sweater and low-heeled shoes. With her neatly styled hair and make-up she looked unremarkably average, the type of person who would blend into a crowd. Hormone therapy had created some breast development; beard growth had been eradicated by electrolysis. The single problem was her voice. This she handled by speaking very softly and quietly, thereby raising its pitch without sounding unnatural.

In her late twenties, Margaret works as a telex-operator in an all-female section. Actually getting and holding on to a job presents a tremendous hurdle for the full-time transvestite, because change from male to female means a change of name and a reconstruction of past history. Thus essential factors, such as references, become instant problems. Margaret resolved this by explaining the situation during her job interview. Her boss was prepared to accept her and not inform her colleagues, but Margaret still has to maintain her guard so as not to make some mistake which might destroy her credibility. She always has to be 'very careful' and she worries a great deal that she'll slip up.

On an everyday basis such dissembling requires unrelieved role-playing at a conscious level, a constant monitoring of performance and an ability to remember exactly what stories and lies have been told. A past biography has to be constructed and, while elements of the real one may be retained, the past has to be obliterated and overlaid with a fictitious personal history that spans many years. A social life must also be invented. Great care must be taken to avoid any overstatement which may be construed as a desire to impress and thereby raise suspicions that the truth is not being told. One only has to imagine a day-to-day work situation where the pretence of being another person has to be maintained, in order to grasp some inkling of the unremitting pressure involved in this type of constant self-monitoring. Margaret summarised her situation by saying, 'I tell a lot of lies, but it's a small price to pay.' Yet clearly the difficulties, while not insurmountable, are immense – from remembering to keep her voice at a modulated pitch to never forgetting to put the toilet seat down after urinating.

Margaret's actual social life revolves around the transvestite subculture, gay clubs and discos. She has a boyfriend whom she met at one of the clubs. Describing him as a 'straight TV' she said, 'Well, he *was* straight till he met me!' However, she wants to relate to him as if their relationship were heterosexual and adamantly refuses to see him when he is cross-dressed. Margaret feels strongly that she is really a woman who has suffered the misfortune of having been placed in the wrong body.

During one conversation with Margaret, she asked what feminism meant, remarking that many feminists display a strong dislike of transsexuals. She felt that this was particularly pernicious because she had suffered a dual form of oppression: as a feminine male when younger, and now as a transsexual. Feminists, she claimed, have misjudged the situation, 'because I really do know what it's like to be a woman'. Moreover, Margaret considered that in her own way she was helping women, because should men attempt to pick her up she would eventually tell them she was a man, which, she insisted, would make them feel small. She did not think this type of behaviour contained a risk of violence, 'Because, you see, they still see me as a woman, so they don't get aggressive.' Rejecting the suggestion that she might be utilising the advantages of masculinity whilst maintaining an external appearance of femininity, Margaret insisted she really was a woman and could, therefore, see the world 'from a woman's standpoint'.

Yvonne

In contrast to Margaret's expression of femininity and demure manner, Yvone undermines her appearance by announcing, 'I never let anyone forget I'm a fella in a frock.' While this may upset those who see themselves as projecting a totally feminine image, Yvonne has few delusions about success and is aware of the impossibility of the task. Notwithstanding a genuine willingness to spend hours counselling and helping those in need, she does not suffer fools gladly and will direct a deflating verbal onslaught at anyone who crosses her. Living for most of the time as a woman, Yvonne's life revolves around transvestism, not simply in a personal sense, but in as much as she has made it a life project. As the main organiser of TV/TS, she is well known in the transvestite world. Although part of her time is devoted to fund-raising for the organisation, and latterly to renovating the new premises, she also offers support to those experiencing difficulties or traumas.

Unlike many transvestites, Yvonne feels no compunction to appear constantly in her feminine role. She would thus arrive at TV/TS as Nick, dressed in old jeans and explaining that it had taken hours to dig the car out of the snow. Known by all her neighbours as both Yvonne and Nick she goes out of her way to help them. On our way to a drag ball after dinner at Yvonne's flat, a neighbour popped out to see how she looked and praised Yvonne's appearance in the manner of a doting mother seeing a favourite daughter off to a party. On her own admission, Yvonne is known in the local shops as 'the nut case of the area', but she has developed a good relationship with the local people and she cultivates this with care. 'Well, there I am on a Saturday morning in me bra and pants and someone knocks on the glass. I know it's alright if they knock on the glass; if they use the knocker it's official – like the rent! So they'll say, "Oh, Yvonne, I'm just going away for the weekend. Can you keep an eye on the place for me?" And I'll say, "Yeah, alright love," and they'll say, "Thanks a lot," and off they go.'

Born in 1928 in the Old Kent Road, Yvonne began to cross-dress in her sisters' clothes at the age of three. Two of her sisters actually joined her in this later, lending clothes and generally assisting her. Yvonne's transvestism has more or less been accepted by both brothers and two of her sisters, but a third remains hostile. Although gay at first, Yvonne married a girlfriend when she got pregnant and she says that her wife accepted the transvestism, although the marriage did not last. After a period in the Merchant Navy, Yvonne spent increasingly more time living as a woman, though she reverted to Nick from time to time in order to get a job. She has worked on the stage and is very much the actress in her day-to-day life, besides being a great raconteur with an anecdote for every occasion. Indeed, she loves to be centre stage and, given her sense of timing and drama, usually is. She claims to be bisexual by choice, but in practice she is predominantly gay, having had only one heterosexual affair in fifteen years.

For Yvonne the problems associated with gender/sex change are always based on an essentially pragmatic view of the situation. For instance, during one meeting at TV/TS she announced to all present, 'Don't kid yourself you're part of normal society because you're not.' In contrast to Margaret, Yvonne claims that there is no such thing as a transsexual, precisely because a man can never become a woman and can never fully comprehend the realities of women's lives. Consequently she pokes fun at those who claim to be 'real women'. 'Go to a transsexual's home on a Monday morning and you'll see him setting off for work like any other man.' Asked to substantiate her claims, Yvonne asserts she was a 'lapsed transsexual' who came within fourteen days of the operation and changed her mind. 'And if you can find me another lapsed transsexual, I'll buy you a bottle of wine.' Yvonne has made TV/TS the major focus of her life, recognising the lack of emotional and social support available to transvestites and transsexuals, as the following incident shows.

Yvonne was driving Babs, a pre-operative transsexual, her boyfriend and myself to a gay bar. Kathy, another transsexual, living full-time as a woman and hoping for reassignment surgery, was going through a period of depression. Yvonne interpreted this as a combination of what she termed 'the six-month period', the time when doubts and uncertainties creep in, and the fact that Christmas was approaching and Kathy was unable to visit her family who were unaware of the gender change. When Babs expressed some misgivings about Kathy's depression, suggesting that she might simply be moping, Yvonne responded by reminding Babs of her own earlier depression. 'You've got to remember that because things have suddenly worked out for you, it doesn't mean that the rest has changed.' Yvonne visited Babs one Christmas and recalled 'finding a very tearful and doped-up Babs because you were left on your own and couldn't go to a family party. *You* were ignored.' Yvonne stressed the need for people to extend a hand of friendship and support especially to those who are experiencing conflict and doubts concerning their newly adopted lifestyle. 'Why does anyone come to that group [TV/TS] except for reassurance?' she concluded.

In summary, Yvonne has adapted to her lifestyle with determination and humour. Her saving grace has been her refusal to take anyone, including herself, completely seriously. Thus, although everything and everyone eventually falls victim to her sarcasm, she has clearly earned the respect of people both within the transvestite group and in her neighbourhood. Unique in the subculture, she lives up to her philosophy of never forgetting that she is 'a fella in a frock', thereby maintaining the best of both worlds. By displaying two gender roles and two personae she avoids much of the pressure associated with the secret double life led by many transvestites. The motivation to remain at a down-to-earth level is strong, obtaining the nurturing that she needs through her nurturance of others.

The fantasy-world transvestite

Transvestism is a fantasy world, a means of becoming another sort of person temporarily while retaining one's own identity, of entering a different and private world which, to some extent, can be of one's own making. Fantasy notwithstanding, the fact remains that transvestites still have to live in the real world, make a living and appear to be no different from anyone else. It is this juxtaposition of fantasy and reality, with the continual switching back and forth, which so often tips the balance, so that an individual may want to stay within his fantasy world, rejecting any other way of life.

Sara

Sara is one such transvestite, claiming to be transsexual, yet spending the bulk of her time, the working week, as a man. Well spoken and articulate, she presents a convincing appearance with her own blonde hair styled into a wavy bob, fairly fashionable clothes and hip padding which gives her a more feminine, if slightly overweight, figure. Although only able to become Sara during her leisure time, she is determined to present a totally convincing image of femininity, so when she won first prize in a drag competition at a ball, she spent all the money on a pair of expensive breast protheses, manufactured for women who have undergone mastectomy operations. While visiting a friend's house often frequented by transvestites, a man had come up to her and said, 'Aha! So you're one of those!' and squeezed the new prothesis. Sara was delighted that he had immediately jumped back in embarrassment, apologising profusely for his 'mistake'.

Sara loves the drag balls and expends much time and effort on making herself elaborate costumes. Dressed in a silver tutu with gossamer wings, sparkling stilettos and plenty of sticky-tape to push up the cleavage, she clearly wanted to be the belle of the ball. She entered one drag competition at a particularly lavish extravaganza in a glittering outfit complete with fake diamond tiara and an exploding Christmas cake which showered the room with sparkles at the appropriate moment, yet she did not appear to enjoy herself and left the ball shortly after being awarded second prize.

Unlike many of the other members of TV/TS, Sara is difficult to communicate with, not so much because she is an unwilling conversationalist – on the contrary – but more on account of her aloofness and distance. It is almost as if she really sees herself as two entirely different people, referring to her male self in the third person. She will mention that Charles can do things that Sara is unable to, presumably because Sara is a 'woman'; it seems as if Sara and Charles comprise two different lives, with Sara being neither fully content nor able to choose between them. (This behaviour change associated with a switch in gender roles is commented on by some of the wives in Chapter 6.)

According to the ways in which notions of normality and abnormality are employed in popular thought, the transvestite falls squarely into the latter category, pursuing an activity regarded as odd, deviant or even perverted. If he does socialise in feminine guise he will tend to do so in an enclosed milieu which is somewhat incestuous and circular, because by being afraid of exclusion themselves, such a group will not actively exclude one another. In many respects the social world of transvestism is somewhat like the psychiatric ward where, even when a patient's behaviour is disruptive, other patients shy away from requesting her/his removal for fear of this censure happening to them.

In social terms the situation is one of people coming together because they share a common, proscribed activity of cross-dressing, but they may have little else in common. This in itself leaves the door wide open for all sorts of deviant behaviour. During research I came across several transvestites who had served prison sentences for offences unrelated to their predilection for feminine clothing. But then the question arises: are these apparently unconnected offences in fact related? Did they commit crimes as a result of having been labelled freaks and perverts because they felt themselves to be social outcasts? Discounting those who had been charged with offences related to soliciting, it is difficult, if not impossible, to establish any sort of causal connnection; to attempt to do so would only leave us unable to explain why so many transvestites have never been involved in crime. Nevertheless, such acts, criminal and deviant, may be rooted in common ground, as in the example of Candy.

Candy

Candy's great passion in life was cars. Unfortunately she had never held a legal driving licence and, unable to resist the temptation of taking and driving away, had been arrested countless times for car theft, besides offences related to insurance, tax and disqualified driving. Candy enjoyed driving while cross-dressed, the car affording a greater level of protection from prying eyes, yet permitting forays in public. When I met Candy she was on bail awaiting trial, the last in a long line of cases for which she expected to receive a prison sentence.

Candy is a transvestite who looks like a man dressed up as a woman. She had destroyed her clothes, wigs and cosmetics several times in 'purges' and, unemployed at the time, she had only a limited wardrobe. Usually she wore charity-shop clothes and balloons filled with water stuffed in a bra. Her blonde wig was the real giveaway because cheap, long wigs are always too perfect to look real.

Like many transvestites, Candy first started cross-dressing when she was five, taking her younger sister's clothes and putting them on at night, after she had gone to bed. 'I don't know *why* I wanted to do it, it just felt nice.' Later Candy would sneak out of the house at night, deriving pleasure from walking round the streets dressed as a girl. This came to an abrupt halt one night when she accidentally kicked over the milk bottles on the front step and was confronted by her parents, horrified at finding their eleven-year-old son dressed in his sister's clothes. Candy was taken to the family doctor who referred her to a psychiatric clinic where she had numerous sessions with a psychiatrist. Whether it was his inability to comprehend the issue or Candy's refusal to co-operate is unclear, but the outcome of the relationship was negative, with the psychiatrist concluding that he could make no progress on the case.

From this experience Candy learned that a greater degree of secrecy was essential. She continued to cross-dress throughout her teens, borrowing her sister's clothes and gradually building up her own collection from jumble sales and charity shops without being discovered. Leaving school and starting work meant that she could now afford to buy new clothes, underwear and wigs, all of which had to be hidden away. It was also around this time that Candy started stealing cars, which eventually led to police involvement. Warnings were followed by fines and correctional training, with each offence being awarded a further disqualification from driving. Candy was living in a bed-sitting room when her arrest for stolen goods resulted in her room being searched. The discovery of a bag of female clothing, underwear, wigs and make-up meant the police had a field day with her, questioning her regularly and harassing her about her transvestism.

At twenty, Candy married her first girlfriend and moved out of London, believing that the combination of marriage, new location and council-house would create a fresh start and a chance to break with the vicious spiral of the past. For a time it seemed that this might come true, but a prolonged bout of unemployment left Candy with time on her hands and little money. To while away the time, she began dressing while her wife was at work, building up a secret collection of clothes once more to replace the ones that she had destroyed earlier, believing that she would no longer need them. Finances were supplemented by car theft. Candy spent much of her time driving around in large, expensive cars dressed as a woman. It was only a matter of time before she was arrested, and in the course of the house being searched Candy's clothes were discovered, to the utter horror of her wife. Candy received an 18-month prison sentence and was immediately divorced by her wife. Prison came as a terrible shock to her. Somehow the possibility had never intruded into her world of fast cars and good living. 'I came out of prison to nothing: no wife, no home, no job – no nothing.'

She returned to London and, having found a job and a room, attempted to stay away from cars. She bought clothes through a mail-order catalogue and spent her evenings and weekends dressed in her newly acquired clothes, watching television alone in her room. By then her parents had rejected her and she'd made no friends at all. Yet she claimed she was happy – she was able to please herself and dress as often as she wished. 'I never had to bother with women, did I – Candy was always there.'

The return of Joe, an old friend and partner in crime, triggered off the thieving anew. Candy left her room and moved into a squat with him, a situation which, although more congenial, restricted the opportunity to cross-dress to hurried sessions in the bathroom when Joe was out. They engaged in an almost daily round of thieving, selling stolen cars and goods and living off the proceeds. But, already known to the police in the area, they were arrested eventually and charged with innumerable offences. At the age of twenty-five, Candy received her second prison sentence, this time for two years.

Candy's story does not readily highlight any links between her criminal activities and her transvestism. But from an early age she had known she was 'different', a feeling that was undoubtedly confirmed by her parents' reaction to discovering her on the doorstep in her sister's clothes. More important than this, though, is Candy's assertion that her parents had been disappointed that she, the second child, had not been a girl. 'To tell the truth, they didn't really want me.' Had she been trying, in the inarticulate manner of early childhood, to be the girl her parents had wanted? This question cannot be answered unequivocally. Perhaps this is the underlying reason for her inability to love anyone except her fantasy creation, her feminine persona. As a male, Candy cares little for the world or for her own well-being, indulging in crime carelessly and recklessly, refusing to contemplate the possibility of arrest or its likely outcome.

These portraits point to the broad diversity of transvestites, dispelling any notion that there must be a 'transvestite type' who can quickly and easily be distinguished from other 'normal' men. There is no particular type of man who cross-dresses, nor any personality profile or background factors which link together these widely differing individuals. Some have experienced childhood events which could be seen as traumatic and, therefore, possible pushing them towards some sort of aberrant behaviour: the loss of a mother at a young age, parents wanting their son to be a girl, for instance. It is impossible, however, to single out a psychological factor and claim with any certainty that this is the root cause of the desire to cross-dress.

Clearly the sub-culture of the transvestite does not cater to any particular type. As we have seen already, all aspects of sexual preference are represented in a mix of dressers and non-dressers. Most transvestites are heterosexual, others homosexual, still others bisexual. And for a self-defined transsexual like Margaret, living full-time as a woman while still biologically a man, what the world would call a homosexual relationship becomes heterosexual for her, because she defines herself as a woman. Then for a transvestite like Candy the need for a sexual relationship with another person is overridden by her self-creation of a synthetic woman. Indeed, those who cross-dress have little in common except that they all experience and express a need to dress as a woman. They also vary greatly in their ability to construct a convincing image of femininity. Some can 'pass' with little difficulty, while others would be 'read' immediately. However, a lack of realism and inability to view oneself objectively is a shortcoming which is by no means restricted to transvestites alone.

The reasons why some men experience this need to dress as a woman are far from clear. Explanations range from laying blame on faulty psycho-sexual development and childhood fears of castration, to the promotion of transvestism as a means to achieve psychic wholeness. Until fairly recently the attention directed towards transvestism has emanated from the medical and psychiatric/psychoanalytic professions, although even here the range and difference of opinion is considerable. It is to medical science and psychology that we now turn to consider the attempted explanations, and cures, for transvestism.

4

The boy can't help it: scientific views of transvestism

'If someone could give me a reason why they do it I'd feel a lot better.'

(Eleanor, married to a transvestite)

In Chapter 2 we saw that transvestism is not a single, unitary process which can be easily identified and categorised into a convenient slot. This is why there has been a tendency towards a proliferation of confused terminology, with transvestism being identified with transsexualism, homosexuality, heterosexuality, fetishism, masochism and dissatisfaction with gender identity/role (a phenomenon known as gender dysphoria syndrome). In popular thought, the transvestite is commonly confused with the transsexual and/or the homosexual, but in medical and psychological research inaccuracy and muddled thinking are also found. Indeed, considering the difficulties encountered in the attempt to locate and define transvestism we may expect research findings to be diverse, particularly if the ways in which ideas about sex and gender have changed during the course of this century are also taken into account.

A key issue here is the part played by gender in the making of sexuality and the ways in which people view their own sexuality and that of others. The transsexual considers his biological sex to be at odds with his gender and thus desires medical and surgical intervention so that he can be reassigned physically to his 'real' gender. Both the drag artist and the transvestite identify as biologically male, but when the drag artist dons female clothing, he does so with the intent of parodying women. In contrast, the transvestite makes no attempt at satire. His ideal is to pass as a woman and to convince others, while, in many cases, deriving sexual satisfaction from wearing feminine attire. In reality these distinctions may blur, as in the case of the transvestite who eventually decides that he is transsexual. But generally the transvestite views his cross-gender activities as periodic and not in contradiction to his biological sex.

The transvestite, then, is concerned only with the culturally defined compononents of the sex-gender interface. For him the usual one-to-one correlation of sex and gender is not the straighforward process assumed by most people. Rather, it is problematic precisely because he desires to assume both genders. While retaining male sex and masculine gender appearance, identity and role, he will also temporarily adopt feminine appearance and, in varying degrees, aspects of the feminine gender identity and role. He will not, however, lose sight of the fact that he is biologically male.

Analyses and subsequent treatment of transvestites by clinicians, psychiatrists and therapists have been largely based on preconceived notions both of gender divisions in general and of transvestism specifically. Research in this area, as in many others in the sciences, has been saturated with unrecognised and unremarked ideologies of gender. As such, it stands as a monument to the often denied existence of bias in the practice of science and its pursuit of truth. In addition it reflects the development of a professional body of 'gender professionals' with a vested interest in the provision of treatment. Such research can be viewed as an archetype of the ways in which unarticulated and taken-for-granted assumptions can push investigation in certain directions, thereby providing concrete supports for the comfortable conceptions of rigid gender demarcation and the presumed pre-eminence of 'normality' versus 'deviance'. The very fact that gender is a cultural variable, socially constructed and therefore malleable, is frequently ignored. Hence transvestites' ideas about femininity and what it means to them become submerged in the researcher's failure to address questions of gender and sexual politics.

Strictly speaking, transvestism is not a medical condition in the sense of it being an illness amenable to diagnosis and cure. But, as with other forms of sexual deviance, it has been subject to the processes of medicalisation whereby, as Talamini (1982) comments, non-conventional sexual behaviour is designated abnormal. By reclassifying unwanted behaviour as a disease, strategies and techniques of intervention aimed at its eradication become permissible and legitimated.[1] Additionally, the overlap and confusion with transsexualism[2] and the medical context of gender-identity clinics has meant that practitioners have tended to approach the subject in accordance with medical paradigms and the desirability of cure. This medicalisation model itself tends to split into two areas of focus: the medico-biological and the medico-psychiatric, spanning a range of 'treatment' from aversion therapy to psychotherapy. Alongside this, the psychoanalytic tradition has been utilised, particularly in the search for causal factors, characterised by variations on the basic theme of childhood psychosexual trauma. Finally there is the socio-psychological approach. Here the focus is directed more towards the social context within a framework of apparently liberal observations and prescriptions. Explanations such as these stand in marked contrast to those which attempt to relate transvestism to considerations of gender and the ways in which gender as a social construct is related to the processes of socio-political control.

Research models will be examined here not simply to place individual researchers into neatly labelled boxes with the express purpose of writing off their findings, but rather because this provides the opportunity to consider the hidden assumptions and unspecified ideas about gender which underlie the development and utilisation of these models. This perspective can prove useful in pinpointing information on transvestism because it directs us to such questions as, for example, why the transvestite has been designated sick, or why he is in need of treatment, whatever that treatment might be. Furthermore, we can ask why so few researchers have considered the question of gender appearance and its significance for the transvestite.

The purpose of looking at these models, then, is to draw out and isolate their underlying and unspoken assumptions concerning gender and sexuality; in short, to consider what Bogdan (1974) has referred to as the 'politics of diagnosis'. This in turn raises questions of the extent to which such models not only become self-fulfilling exercises in 'finding' predetermined 'facts', but also become ways of upholding, and even strengthening, prevailing ideologies of gender.

A suitable case for treatment?

Within medical research, transvestism has a comparatively short history, the term first being used in 1910 by the sexologist Magnus Hirschfield. Early approaches tended to view transvestism as having constitutional causes, a view only slightly modified by Benjamin, an endocrinologist and specialist in gender disorders. He argues that the basis of transvestism is primarily physical with psychological factors playing a secondary role only:

> Is it not logical to assume that a constitutionally robust central nervous system can withstand psychological traumata easier than a delicate one? (1953, p. 13)

Treatment is thus defined as endocrinological, i.e. hormonal therapy for masculinisation (which, incidentally, has no apparent success in curing transvestism and often intensifies its frequency by boosting libido). But Benjamin also refers to the necessity of 'treating' society and of education for tolerance and understanding. This attitude may be considered radical for the early 1950s, but a decade and a half later he was still stressing endocrinological factors, even in the pre-natal stage of development. Even later, and with more doubtful logic, Buhrich (1977) has argued that the causes of transvestism must be constitutional rather than environmental because it appears to be exclusively confined to men.

Significantly, Benjamin emphasises the necessity of the 'correct fit' between sex and gender, a theme which is constantly reasserted throughout research into transvestism. Such thinking is invariably located within a rigid demarcation between normality and abnormality, entailing a view of deviance as something which is indulged in only by a pathological minority. However, when a biologically based analysis is employed, the label of 'bad' is, in effect, sidestepped, precisely because, within this model, the transvestite becomes the victim of some malfunction. Thus he becomes 'sad', as opposed to irretrievably 'bad'.

This mode of explanation is also found in the work of Desavitsch (1958) and Armstrong (1958), but while the former simply presses home the case for tolerance in the face of biological mishap (in this instance, chromosomal), Armstrong offers greater insight into the role played by the expert in the politics of diagnosis. In a paper presented to a medical symposium on chromosomal sex, Armstrong discusses a transvestite case history which, he claims, is 'very typical'. In fact, the description of the case closely resembles the typical model of the transsexual in so far as this transvestite had claimed that he was 'really' a woman; that he hated his genitals and desired their removal; that he did not want a sexual relationship with a woman, and that he wished to live full-time as a woman. While claiming that the cause of transvestism is genetic, Armstrong's paper provides an excellent example of the way in which 'data' – in this instance, the case study – may be used to support preconceived ideas. It also shows the extent to which the expert's interpretation of events may totally override and thus invalidate the patient's definition of the situation.

Of course, one of the problems with research carried out in the 1950s was the diagnostic confusion of transvestism (or transvestitism as it was commonly called) and transsexualism. For instance, both Armstrong and Hamburger *et al.* (1953) present case studies of transvestite men who would nowadays be included under the transsexual rubric. However, changes in diagnostic criteria notwithstanding, an assumption underlying all biologically directed research in this field is that gender disorders stem from somatic malfunction. Thus gender becomes *nothing more* than the visible expression of correct biological functioning, and deviation from the sex-gender fit becomes abnormal, a biological aberration. Quite simply, this model is based on biological determinism, a crude model of human behaviour which argues that the social, cultural and psychological facets of society are little more than reflections of biological imperatives. Thus, just as the early criminologists attempted to prove that criminal behaviour was the result of chromosomal abnormalities, so the medico-biological model claims that transvestism is a manifestation of hormonal or chromosomal malfunction.

While biological determinism may have made little headway in the analysis of transvestism, the untheorised and unarticulated notions of normality and abnormality contained in it are not limited solely to this model. The whole medico-psychological approach to transvestism is, in varying degrees, predicated on such notions. Thus ensuing treatment has frequently exhibited what Szasz (1973) coined 'correctional zeal'. No longer the hapless victims of biological malfunction, transvestites have been depicted as the sad, or even mad, victims of socio-psychological maladjustment who could, nevertheless, be treated successfully, thereby enabling them to enjoy the benefits of conformity. As King has argued:

this model encompasses all those views which, whilst accepting the behaviour as indicative of an essence, deny its tenability and seek to eliminate it by therapy, punishment, proscription or whatever. (1984, pp. 46–7)

While the greater part of socio-psychological research has focused upon gender role conditioning, this notion of maladjustment also provided the link with strategies of behavioural modification – various techniques which rose to prominence in the 1950s and 1960s and often employed aversion or avoidance therapy (either chemical or electrical), particularly in the field of sexual deviance. Not noted for its success, aversion therapy rests on two major assumptions: willingness on the part of the patient; and the tenets of behaviourism, which claim that human behaviour can be altered by means of conditioning.

One of the problems implicit in the use of aversion therapy for transvestism is that it is unclear from the outset just what is being treated. Bond and Evans (1967) report on two cases of aversion treatment through electric shock of teenage underwear fetishists, whereby avoidance of women's underwear was successfully established. In such avoidance programmes where the aim is to bring about the extinction of a form of behaviour, the transvestite is little more than an object of study who may, of course, have been wrongly diagnosed. Thus Brierley (1979) observes that most aversion therapy treats only for fetishism, which may not necessarily be present in a transvestite's use of female clothing. Hence the largely unsuccessful outcome of any of the reported case studies.[3] It is also worth noting that the underwear fetishism in one of the cases only appeared after he had been 'successfully' treated for exhibitionism.

An example of aversion therapy based on the classical Pavlovian conditioning model is provided by Pearce (1963). While admitting that his approach is based on learning theory and thus treats the symptoms (the learned responses which, by the time of treatment, have become habitual) as the neurosis itself, he inadvertently demonstrates the crude nature of aversion-based techniques.

Pearce administered drugs (apomorphine to induce vomiting and dexidrine to prevent sleep) during forty instances of cross-dressing by each of eight transvestite patients. He concedes that a major problem with the use of apomorphine lies in timing the relationship between the conditioned stimulus and the unconditioned response from which the aversion response is to develop. Nevertheless, Pearce claims that, with the exception of one patient who was suffering from a physiological brain disorder which may have impaired learning capacity, all the patients 'improved or were cured' (p. 183.)

Given the lack of definition it is difficult to assess just what this apparent success meant to the transvestites themselves. Did aversion therapy decondition the fantasy, the cross-dressing, or both? Moreover, from Pearce's description of the programme it would seem that an emotional disturbance was established in reaction to the unpleasant effects of the treatment. Thus the question arises: did the therapy actually establish extinction or merely an avoidance response? Without a control group or a follow-up study it is impossible to ascertain the long-term effects of the therapy or Pearce's claims for improvement or cure. The methods and effects of drug-based programmes such as this have been described by Talamini (1982) as 'degrading'.

Working along similar lines, Barker (1966) has also suggested that the transvestite presents a behavioural pattern which is highly suitable for treatment. He too claims a successful outcome in the application of both chemical and electric-shock therapy, but as he fails to spell out his criteria for measuring this success it is impossible to evaluate his findings. The lack of methodological safeguards is not unique to this case. Taylor and McLachlan (1962, 1963) base their observations on a study of ten transvestites, all convicted prisoners. Ball (1967, 1968) attempts conclusions on the basis of a study of six transvestites, all of whom were diagnosed as maladjusted, with low IQ and impaired verbal ability.

The increasing discredit accorded such approaches within the field of social science is reflected in the history of research into transvestism, and as these models gradually declined in popularity so notions of social, psychological and sexual maladjustment came to prominence, retaining in some cases the desirability of cure but also turning towards prevention. In Weeks's (1981) outline of the transition from behavioural modification models to social delinquency models, we find a close parallel with the development of research into transvestism. The transvestite may be sad, or even mad, but this is pre-eminently because he is 'sick', suffering from what Beigel describes as psychosexual maladjustment, stemming from painful childhood experiences which have arrested his development. It is here that we find elements of what may be called the dominant/absent parent syndrome. Beigel (1969) argues that, as a child, the transvestite felt alienated from his father and sought to please his mother by engaging in 'feminine' activities. Consequently he is unable to accept his masculinity in later life. Transvestism, he argues, is a 'psychopathological state' which requires cure by psychotherapy because it causes unhappiness. Even leaving aside Beigel's unquestioning use of 'feminine' and 'masculine', it is abundantly clear that his understanding of transvestism is based on the assumption that the individual can achieve happiness or satisfaction only by conformity to existing social norms. Labelling the transvestite as 'sick' simultaneously promotes the idea of individual pathology whilst relegating the significance of social factors to the background.

Undoubtedly transvestism does cause conflict and unhappiness for some transvestites as well as for their partners. Thus some means of alleviating this suffering is called for. Indeed, transvestism may well stem from problems associated with early childhood experiences. Nevertheless, we find that unspoken assumptions concerning the nature of normality and conformity, femininity and masculinity abound in these 'liberal' medico-psychiatric models of the 1960s. This results in contradiction: while the importance of socialisation is stressed, the fact that masculinity and femininity are social constructs and not timeless entities is wholly glossed over.

Brown (1960) goes along with an early-socialisation-experiences explanation for the causes of transvestism but, in contrast, claims that as psychotherapy does not necessarily work in this instance we must consider preventive measures. Such measures, he claims, would entail the provision of strong parental figures in the child's early years who will love him as a male and encourage his development along strictly masculine lines. Just how this might be effected is unclear, but certainly visions of unannounced visits by the Department for Social Welfare and Gender Role Conformity spring to mind! In a later paper (1967) Brown argues that as transvestism is a behaviour pattern learned in the early stages of infancy and childhood (0–3 years), extinction through behaviour modification is extremely difficult. There is a shift of emphasis here from cure to prevention based on a notion of 'correct' gender role conditioning which ignores the relationship between gender stereotyping and social control.

Green (1974), a recognised authority in the field of sexual deviance, presents a classic formulation of the familial/environmental breakdown syndrome. As the family is the primary locus for the provision of role models for children, transvestism can be traced to insufficient disapproval, or even encouragement, of inappropriate gender behaviour. This may be exacerbated by an over-influence of girls in peer groups and/or parental protection from 'rough boys'. Green does refer to sexist society, but is reasonable enough to define his role as one of helping individuals to adapt to society's demands. However, later writings (1978) offer an indication of his underlying focus when he reports that homosexual and transsexual parents do not raise psychosexually disturbed children:

> The daughter is feminine and heterosexual . . . the boy is not considered a 'sissy' . . . Their identity is reflected in the fact that the boy wants to be a daddy when he grows up and the girl wants to be a mommy. (pp. 694–5).

Comments such as these extend beyond a reassertion of the primacy of gender division, the nuclear family and the naturalness of it all. They raise the spectre of manipulative control through institutions generally known as 'gender identity clinics'. While possibly providing a service to self-referred adults, the modification and correction of 'inappropriate' gender behaviour in children again raises questions about social control and gender stereotyping.[4]

The assortment of conflicting factors contained in the medico-psychiatric model of the familial-environment process is typified by Randell (1975). Referring to the high incidence of 'environmental factors' in the biographies of transvestites, he cites stern, rigid fathers; absent, dead or weak fathers; overprotective mothers; and broken homes. As a result one can only wonder why the whole male population does *not* exhibit some manifestation of transvestism! As Mackenzie (1978) observes, the lack of objective criteria for the identification of gender discomfort leaves the field wide open. Thus the spotlight may pick on an overly close mother in one case, a neighbourhood of girls in another and a seductive babysitter in the next. Such indecision in the location of causal factors is, however, less characteristic of Storr (1964) who, in placing the blame squarely on the mother, must be unparalleled in his published hatred of women:

Most people will know from their own experience of cases in which a mother has possessively clung to a son, destroying his independence, blackmailing him into staying with her, preventing his marriage. Such mothers are indeed witches, who have stolen their son's masculinity. (p. 63)

Having referred to this mother figure as a witch, Hecate, he then moves on to quote from 'Maleus Maleficarum', the medieval tract used to persecute and murder thousands of women said to be witches. Here, then, the transvestite is both sick and sad, the victim of an evil mother, herself sick but also mad. The focus on infantile and early childhood experience, together with the emphasis placed upon the mother as a central figure in the development of psychosexual maladjustment, demonstrates close similarities to the psychoanalytical approach to transvestism. Indeed, Storr's work may be seen a bridging the medico-psychiatric and psychoanalytical approaches to the subject.

Psychoanalysis and the 'phallic woman'

The stress placed on the importance of the first years of life and subsequent symptoms which may emerge as a result of conflict and trauma, is a theme common to explanations of behaviour from juvenile delinquency to sexual psychopathy. Much of this thinking derives from the direct influence and infiltration of modified or even distorted strands of psychoanalysis, an approach which focuses, predictably enough, on the sexual aspect of transvestism, defining it as a 'perversion'.[5] Female clothing comes to represent the mother in symbolic form. Thus by cross-dressing, it is argued, the transvestite is able to recreate the symbiotic relationship he once enjoyed with his mother and thereby allay his fear of castration.

Transvestism is interpreted as a symptom of the failure to resolve oedipal conflict. Segal (1965) argues that it is a form of defence against homosexuality, 'a perversion of choice whenever a homosexual need cannot be gratified or, because of shame, must be avoided' (p. 216). If this is the case, it becomes difficult to explain the existence of the homosexual transvestite, a point recognised earlier by Barahal (1953) who rejects the suggestion of neurotic defence, claiming that homosexuality is, in itself, a multi-determined sympton of neurosis.

A classic formulation of the psychoanalytical angle on transvestism and the pride of place attributed to the penis is found in the work of Fenichel (1954). Defining transvestism as sexual perversion instead of neurosis, he argues alongside Freud that all perversions are connected to the castration complex and thus revolve around infantile activities which will allay anxiety. The unconscious mechanisms underlying fetishism, passive homosexuality and transvestism are similar in so far as the homosexual has no regard for someone who lacks a penis. The fetishist denies that people without penises exist, and the transvestite (or the exhibitionist) tries to refute the possibility of castration. By identifying himself as a phallic woman, that is by becoming a woman with a penis, he appeals to both parents for love. To his father he's announcing, 'I am just as beautiful as my mother'. To his mother he is either denying that his desire for her places his penis in jeopardy or he is demanding that she love him as she loves his sister. The centre-stage role assigned here to the penis is underlined by Fenichel's claim that the female transvestite in fact covets a penis of her own.

In contrast, Stoller (1976) offers a modification of Freud's theory of psychosexual development, by rejecting the notion that a clear-cut distinction between masculinity and feminity does not occur until puberty, and creating an earlier stage where gender differentiation occurs before the onset of oedipal conflict. It is at this earlier stage that the boy, in contrast to the girl, has to separate himself from the mother in order to overcome his sense of oneness with the female. If, however, the mother fails to encourage his masculinity this separation will not be completed successfully. Transvestite behaviour then symbolises a merging with the mother while simultaneously permitting a separation from her by enabling him to retain the power of maleness – the hidden penis. Stoller insists that transvestism is fetishistic behaviour which stems not only from the role of the mother in failing to facilitate the child's masculinity but also from the role of the father:

> While frightening and distant, these men introduce another quality into the relationship: they have rare moments of capricious tenderness with their sons. And so the boys hunger for their fathers, loving them despairingly with an almost sexual tinge . . . the yearning is so intense, the hope that he might be won so close, that an eroticised state of tension and frustration builds up. (1971, p. 231)

This results in the creation of the 'phallic woman', a term coined by Stoller which, while intended to encapsulate the fetishistic nature of cross-dressing, is also suggestive of the imagery found in transvestite pornography:

> the presence of the penis sensed beneath the woman's garments is exciting. They never quite forget the trick: the hidden penis. (Ibid)

A similar perspective is also found in Storr's work (1964). Although not overtly psychoanalytical, he incorporates the notion of the phallic woman into his model of psychosexual inadequacy, arguing that the transvestite identifies with her as a means of compensating for his lacking relations with women. The fault, of course, lies entirely with the mother. Stoller also attributes the development of male transsexualism to the mother who feminises her son to satisfy her need for revenge on men. Men in general, he argues, face problems in developing masculinity and show hostility towards women on account of 'having been born, reared, and therefore, frustrated by a woman' (1968, p. 226).

Despite Stoller's depiction of the transvestite as a phallic woman, he refutes the primacy of the penis claimed by Freud and subsequently by Fenichel. He interprets castration anxiety not simply as fear of genital loss but also as the loss of male identity which is the 'core of one's being' (1976, p. 73). Cross-dressing can serve to allay this double-sided threat. By dressing in women's clothes the transvestite can redress the balance and prove that women cannot overpower him, thereby becoming a victor rather than a victim. By possessing the best of both sexes, he becomes better than a woman. By rejecting female reproductive power and sexuality, she is no longer a threat to him.

Stoller frequently refers to 'masculine development' and 'pleasure in masculinity' but fails to explain the meaning attached to these terms. He assumes that transvestism springs from a badly constructed psyche; if the misalignment is corrected or removed all will fall into place, i.e. a 'normal' pattern. Thus, in this respect, he falls into the same trap as those who call for 'correct' gender role conditioning. How can we socialise or condition for something when we are unsure of how it is defined and constituted or, indeed, if we even want it? The desire to develop diagnostic criteria and thus, presumably, the appropriate treatment would seem to override the need for any discussion or clarification of key terminology, most particularly notions of normality and abnormality, femininity and masculinity.

Thus far, it can be seen that the transvestite has been defined as a case for treatment, either by methods which will extinguish learned patterns of behaviour or by the practice of psychotherapy or psychoanalysis. Of these methods probably the most success has been associated with psychotherapy, a process which can be time-consuming and expensive and, as Wise (1979) demonstrates in a case study, can lead only to symptom resolution, not cure; there may be recurrence in the future. The resounding failure of such interventionist approaches partially explains the stress placed on prevention, a claim which demonstrates the lack of awareness concerning the socio-political constituents of gender construction and which, furthermore, rests on reactionary support for traditional, oppressive ideas about gender divisions.

Stoller, however, eventually concedes that strict formulae cannot be applied to the explanation of sexual behaviour in general and to perversion in particular. Despite his frequent attempts to codify and establish causes, he admits that little is known about the roots and mechanisms of human sexual behaviour after the inputs of heredity, constitution and environment, and that we need to know 'what people do, what they think they are doing, what they think while they are doing it, and what they think of what they are doing' (1976, p. 45). In this respect, at least, it would seem that Stoller is showing some recognition of the need for a more socially orientated framework which might allow subjects to speak for themselves and offer their own definitions of the situation. While such an approach is theoretically within the capacities of a socio-psychological analysis, what we find, in fact, is that many of the shortcomings of the approaches outlined above are simply reproduced.

From individual to society

It might be expected that explanations directed towards specifically social considerations would offer greater cognisance of the ways in which gender is moulded by its social context. However, the liberalism enshrined in many such approaches requires, at the very least, a degree of caution. Within this we find a dual focus displayed. Attention is paid to the confines of masculinity, and thus, in contrast to psychoanalysis, the practice of cross-dressing is, by and large, desexualised. Additionally there exists the attempt to stir the social conscience by depicting society, and not the individual, as sick. The transvestite becomes the outcast of an intolerant society, a harmless, stigmatised victim of reactionary attitudes.

In contrast to this latter view, Buckner (1970) provides an example of a social psychological perspective which substitutes sociosexual for psychosexual categories. In effect, he presents a sort of sociologised psychoanalysis which retains the significance attached to sexual behaviour. Rejecting biologically based explanations, he suggests that transvestism represents a means of protection. Whereas the psychoanalysts define cross-dressing as fetishism, a device to allay castration fears, Buckner argues that transvestism protects the individual from the social reality of interpersonal relations by replacing it with the 'synthetic reality' of the 'synthetic dyad'. In other words, it enables the transvestite to retreat from outside reality and create a kind of facsimile within which he can achieve sexual gratification; the substitution of synthetic sexual relations for human ones. Thus we have the substitution of the ersatz for the real; the controllable for the unpredictable. Buckner makes a salient point but doesn't seem to wonder why some men, but not women, want to create this kind of fantasy figure. By ignoring sexual politics Buckner fails to follow his argument through.

While psychoanalysis has tended to categorise transvestism as a primarily sexual phenomenon excluding, for the most part, any consideration of gender, we find that the social psychological models generally focus more on gender than on sexuality. For instance, the 'gender disorder' school moves to the opposite extreme and excludes all reference to sexual pleasure. Brierley (1979) argues that the connection between sex and gender is often misunderstood, that the two terms have become conflated and thus gender inversion is taken to indicate sexual perversion. He refers to transvestism as a manifestation of 'gender dysphoria', a discomfort with the appropriate gender role. This accords with the pro-transvestite literature which generally ignores or even denies the existence of sexual pleasure in cross-dressing.

The term 'gender dysphoria syndrome', coined probably in the 1970s, attempts to convey the relativity of the phenomenon and the fact that most people have some experience of it in varying degrees.[6] Money (1974), however, refers to 'gender identity disorder' with all the implications of reordering along 'correct' lines. He thereby retains the importance attached to treatment, a reflection perhaps of his work at Johns Hopkins University's gender clinic.

Brierley portrays the transvestite as someone who is 'successful' in a masculine role but also 'nurtures a capacity to slip into a feminine role', suggesting that this may stem from an over-evaluation of both gender roles (1979, p. 21). The basis of his observation is that transvestites tend to be strongly masculine in the male role and very feminine in the female role. Brierley rests his claims on the notion that gender roles are learned patterns of behaviour. He rejects both aversion techniques and psychoanalysis for the explanation and treatment of transvestism in an attempt to avoid the usual focus on the transvestite himself and also to account for the role played by social responses to such behaviour.

Undoubtedly an examination of the social responses to deviant gender appearance/identity can be revealing. Immediately we have to ask why deviation from masculine appearance is met with much greater disapprobation than deviation from the feminine. In some respects typical social responses tend to reaffirm Marcuse's (1965) claim that hedonistic sexual pleasure, as opposed to utilitarian function, is anathema to the social order. The representation of deviant behaviour, especially sexual deviance, as sick and thereby symptomatic of inadequacy has provided a convenient mechanism for rationalising the necessity and desirability of treatment. But simply to reverse this process and label society as 'sick' would seem only to replace one form of myopia with another. The insight of Marcuse's analysis has been distorted in precisely this way by West (1974). His pleas for tolerance and reform of 'sex laws' typify would-be-liberal, woolly-minded thinking. In calling for the removal of legal restraint on activities (such as transvestism) which are not proven harmful to others, it seems that West imagines that legislative changes will suddenly 'make it alright', whereas in fact we come no closer to an understanding of the phenomenon in hand and the problems which it may, or may not, entail for those concerned. As will be seen in later chapters, some wives of transvestites suffer a considerable psychological strain, even if they put on a brave face in public. While this in itself is not sufficient reason to retain repressive laws, certainly no support for the 'harmless until proven otherwise' dictum as propounded by West can be found here. Bringing it all out in the open is no failsafe formula for problem-solving.

The case for tolerance, even at the expense of wives, is prevalent in pro-transvestite literature. Thompson (1951) asserts that transvestism is symptomatic of emotional disturbance caused by faulty socialisation, but completely avoids the question of just what comprises 'good' socialisation. It is, however, in the writing of Prince (a transvestite himself) that we find the transvestite presented as 'the most perfect example of human kind'.[7] Prince and Bentler (1972) offer one of the few analyses of transvestites that is not selected from those opting for treatment. Notwithstanding this, the necessarily quantitative focus of a mailed questionnaire (conducted with subscribers to *Transvestia*, a magazine run by Prince) provides little in the way of informative data, with one notable exception. In most of the literature, familial processes are cited in one way or another as primary causal factors in the inception of transvestism. Yet Prince and Bentler could find no conclusive evidence for this. It could be argued that such patterns are typical only of those presented to medical and psychiatric personnel, or even that the transvestite's own assessment of the causes of his behaviour is at odds with published diagnoses, but the evidence submitted in this survey is necessarily partial. Thus it is impossible to draw any conclusion from it.

In an earlier paper (1957) Prince argues that transvestism occurs on a social level only; that the transvestite desires to be the recipient of attitudes and behaviour typically displayed towards women and that such behaviour has nothing to do with sexuality or sexual desires. The idealising contained in such argument warrants little comment; suffice to say that Prince would appear to be unaware of the disadvantages accruing to women in sexist society. A theme common to all Prince's writings is the denial of sexual pleasure through cross-dressing. But given the fact that he devotes a great deal of space to encouraging tolerance and understanding on the part of wives, it is only to be expected that sexual aspects will be played down and emphasis given to the notion that, in all other respects, the transvestite is a 'normal', 'masculine' male.[8] This kind of 'normalisation' of the transvestite is especially prevalent in the pro-transvestite literature.

What we find, then, is that the more socially orientated focus on transvestism in fact splits into two somewhat different approaches. On the one hand there is the recognition of some sort of problem or disorder – the inability to deal successfully with sexual relationships, or dissatisfaction with gender identity and role, the wish to experience and act out both genders. On the other we have the deflection of blame from individual to society, the claim that there is very little wrong with the transvestite, that it is society which is at fault, that it is sick and intolerant. As a result the transvestite becomes normalised. However, none of these approaches offers much in the way of analysis of the dynamics of gender or the role this plays in the maintenance of division and control. As such they merely add another prop to those who would deny the existence of sexual politics.

So where does all this leave us in our attempt to understand transvestism? Sadly, it must be said, not much the wiser. Faced with a plethora of conflicting views, it is only too easy to pick holes, to put up various arguments only to knock them down. Rather than take each approach in turn and engage in this somewhat pointless exercise, it will be more productive to consider some of the themes which are either characteristic features or, conversely, are conspicuous by their absence.

First there is the marked attempt to search for causal factors. This is logical in the context of approaches which conceptualise transvestism as a form of sexual deviance. The history of sexology is riddled with debates concerning the cause of this, that and the other. Yet the reasons why a person becomes a transvestite can no more be explained than the process of becoming heterosexual rather than homosexual. And even if this could be explained – the causes identified and pinpointed with diagnostic clarity – what would we do with the information? The possibilities and ramifications of enforced conformity, not simply the prevention of transvestism, are endless and point to yet another mode of authoritarian control in everyday life. Already there are documented cases of children being whisked off to gender-identity clinics because they have failed to display the 'correct' gender role behaviour.[9]

However, while the seemingly endless search for causes may have little to offer, one cannot ignore the fact that although some transvestites are distressed by their behaviour and do seek some sort of help, the majority do not seek treatment precisely because they derive a great deal of pleasure from their activities. Of those who do request help, the majority do so as a result of marital or familial pressures. This comes from the fact that transvestism is not merely a private form of behaviour relevant only to the transvestite himself. The claim that it is a completely harmless activity is not strictly true: it can, and does, affect others, most particularly the women married to transvestites. Thus it can impose difficulties and conflict. In short, there is a need for sympathetic support and help, both for transvestites and their partners, especially since treatment would appear to be short on sympathy and lacking in effectiveness.

In fact what we find is that where transvestism has been subjected to the process of medicalisation by practitioners employing traditional and unarticulated notions of gender, it becomes an illness to be treated and cured. Where the transvestite is depicted as the victim of a sick society there exists little more than a plea for tolerance. Either way the notion of sickness underlies the various conceptualisations of transvestism, which leads to the question: why should a man who desires to adopt a feminine image from time to time, thereby temporarily relinquishing masculinity, be designated sick in some way? But we also need to ask why some men wish to abrogate their claim to primary status masculinity and adopt the trappings of the second sex. Given the secondary location of femininity, it is not surprising that men who embrace it are labelled pathological.

Undoubtedly a factor linking this lack of agreement concerning the causes of transvestism and the lack of successful methods of treatment and cure is the continual failure to confront issues of gender and the ways in which gender is manifested within a specifically social context. We continually meet with variations on the theme of masculinity/femininity, yet we are never offered any sort of explanation of what these terms mean within the framework of the particular research programme.

It may be argued that to all intents and purposes the transvestite is a 'normally masculine' male. But from the wife's point of view he may lose all masculinity (as shown by Susan, for example, in Chapter 6). The research models outlined here contain, albeit covertly in many instances, direct reflections of oppressive constructions of gender. Perhaps, as Brierley (1979) suggests, a more rewarding enterprise would be to examine social responses to transvestism rather than to continue the fruitless search for causes. Certainly the failure of research in this latter area has led to the deployment of measures incorporating reactionary modes of social control directed toward maintaining the inviolability and primacy of the idea of masculinity. As Talamini (1982) observes, 'psychiatrists and physicians continue to be enforcement agents of social norms' (p. 54). Concern with social responses to transvestism may well have more to offer and broaden our understanding of the ways in which gender divisions confine and restrict. We also need to consider whether there is an obverse: does transvestism have an effect on gender? By flaunting the conventions of gender can transvestism have a role in breaking down the gender divide?

Transvestism and women

'They think that women have a better life than men, but it's totally untrue. You can't escape from pain and problems, can you? You've still got to face up to them whether you wear a skirt or trousers.'

(June, married to a transvestite)

If all appearance were reality the world we live in would probably be a very different place. As it is, we construct images of ourselves, projecting them through our appearance, and in this respect the transvestite is no different. He too creates an image and hopes that it will be convincing in the eyes of others. The difference lies in the fact that his image is socially unacceptable and is generally greeted with a response emanating from the shock-horror end of the scale.

At this point we need to consider feminist attitudes to dress. Clearly there is no coherent feminist party line, nor am I attempting to invent one, but there are certain themes which have emerged during the Second Wave of feminism. One of these revolves around the idea of the 'natural'. Janet Radcliffe Richards (1980) sees the equation of 'natural' with 'real' as underlying feminist contempt for the adornment of fashion and cosmetics because they create a false impression, they comprise deception. If we take this and apply it to transvestism it could be argued that men must be 'natural' men and that transvestism is just another facet of the deception of the feminine. But such an argument contains two flaws. First, it assumes that all feminists reject the artifice of fashion and thus, by implication, any woman who does not cannot be a feminist. Second, it is not simply a question of dissemblance, because in the western world *all* appearance is constructed. Regardless of whether we are talking about high fashion, anti-fashion or non-fashion, all appearances are making statements in one way or another. Commonly feminist groupings have utilised some pastiche of imagery to project the statements they want to make and thus an alternative fashion is set up as morally and politically superior.

However, the transvestite displays a marked tendency to use a notion of femininity which precludes any possibility of breaking down the barriers of gender division. As Elizabeth Wilson points out, 'certain styles of female dress are held to signal sexuality in such a way that invites sexual harassment, makes women vulnerable' (1985, p. 235). More often than not, this is the image that is parodied by the transvestite. Nevertheless, if we accept Wilson's thesis that fashion is a system of symbols and that clothes play an essential part in the production of self, is it then a contradiction to argue that what transvestites are doing is politically unacceptable or even morally wrong? In other words, if it is acceptable to argue, as Wilson does, that feminist concerns with naturalness and authenticity are inappropriate and that interest in fashion and playing with fashion are not beyond the political pale, can transvestites then be criticised for *their* choice?

It could be said that when the transvestite cross-dresses he is engaging in fantasy, a variation on Wilson's notion of playing around with fashion. Everyone has fantasies, some more socially acceptable than others, but then not everyone plays them out. The easy solution would be simply to include transvestism under the heading of harmless fantasy and wish fulfilment and leave it at that, but this would be unacceptable for two reasons. Firstly, transvestism is not always a privatised and personal pastime. Partners may be involved and, as shown in Chapter 6, they can experience distress. Secondly, and from a feminist standpoint, the one-way traffic of cross-dressing from male to female cannot be construed as merely accidental. Why do some men wish to masquerade as women to the extent of passing as women in public, and why do they derive some sort of satisfaction from it, be it sexual or as a release from tension? What can this tell us about the relative statuses of femininity and masculinity in a society where masculinity is accorded pride of place? For these two reasons at least, it is important to attempt to arrive at some sort of assessment of transvestism.

Feminist responses

Feminist work has tended to focus, not surprisingly, on the position of women in society and, as yet, there is not a great deal of work on men. Feminists have argued that their proper sphere of work is women and that men can work on themselves, but as only a minority have responded to this challenge there are few publications which deal directly with male heterosexuality. Narrowing this field down even further, the feminist response to transvestism is negligible, with a little more attention directed towards transsexualism, largely as a result of Janice Raymond's ground-breaking polemic, *The Transsexual Empire*. Although transsexualism differs from transvestism in significant ways (see Chapter 2), it will be useful to examine some of Raymond's arguments, especially as she claims that transsexualism highlights issues which extend beyond its own parameters to a critique of so-called 'normal' society.

In the previous chapter it was suggested that medico-psychiatric approaches to transvestism display a tendency to treat femininity and masculinity as fixed categories possessing an essential reality of their own. Raymond extends this argument, claiming that the medical management of transsexualism amount to nothing more than a 'band aid' solution in a repressive society where the façade of liberal tolerance is more apparent than real. Surgical intervention into gender disorders is a mechanism of patriarchal control which functions to avoid any confrontation with its own rigid notions of gender division. Raymond focuses entirely on male-to-female transsexualism, claiming that its obverse is nothing more than tokenism. Rejecting psychological and family-based approaches to the etiology of transsexualism, Raymond takes as 'First Cause' patriarchal society with its attendant gender roles. Transsexualism is simply the 'logical conclusion' of patriarchy, and thus it is society, and not the transsexual, which must be changed. However, transsexualism has been taken over by an 'empire' of medical personnel, clinicians and therapists, and thus any 'initial protest against sex-role stereotyping . . . becomes short circuited' (1980, p. 31). In short, she is saying that those who attempt to break through the barriers set up by the cultural definitions of masculinity do not require behaviour modification through therapy nor do they need to resort to surgical reassignment. Rather they could become some sort of political vanguard in the battle against patriarchy.

Raymond is, of course, talking specifically about those who want to change their biological sex as well as their gender appearance. Could her arguments also apply to transvestism? Because transvestism also breaks the 'rules' of gender does it amount to a potential attack on gender role conformity, if only by drawing attention to the existence and man-made nature of those rules? One problem here is that Raymond herself does not in the end see these rules as man-made, as the artificial construction of a sexist society. She seems to be working with a fixed notion of gender, seeing it as a natural part of sexual difference and not a cultural creation. She accuses transsexuals of 'colonizing' women's bodies and 'invading' women's minds because, post-surgery, some have become lesbian feminists. In 'colonizing' lesbian-feminist groups they are practising deception, because they are not women, they are deviant males. Further, women who accept post-operative transsexuals as women have a dubious commitment to feminism. Sandra McNeill (1982) agrees that such entry into feminism is a threat to the autonomy of women by men who have been castrated and who wear women's clothes, but have not grown up as women, and, like Raymond, she concludes that 'they should fight the system, not change their own bodies' (p. 83).

Both Raymond and McNeill assert that there is something essential about femininity, and, by implication, masculinity, which cannot be changed. But if it cannot be changed, why do they then assert that transsexuals would do better to fight gender stereotyping? They are suggesting that it is impossible for a person to change gender along with physical sex, yet at the same time they call for the collapse of rigid gender divisions. They cannot have it both ways. Either gender roles must be attacked on all fronts in the interests of bringing about the demise of patriarchy or, as the apologists for patriarchy would argue, gender division is just as biologically necessary as sexual differentiation for the survival of the species.

In attacking post-operative transsexuals for joining lesbian-feminist groups, Raymond seems to be suggesting that there is something crucial about femininity which cannot be acquired or learned, that such groups must be the preserve of 'real' women. While this particular problem does not arise with transvestism, since the construction of femininity remains superficial and temporary, the underlying questions are relevant. Does cross-dressing in and of itself attack the citadel of patriarchy – gender division? The concept of gender discomfort, which has frequently been used to describe the transvestite, could also be applied to feminists. But when Raymond points out that we are not provided with gender-identity clinics and therapy for gender role oppression she misses the point, because feminists who challenge such oppression and live their lives accordingly are not attempting to be men, either in the sense of gender appearance or in terms of becoming physically male.

There is a contradiction in Raymond's assessment of transsexualism: medical management upholds patriarchy and the transsexual would do better to fight oppressive gender divisions: but there is some essential component of femaleness and femininity which cannot be constructed surgically or culturally. Conversely, as Alice Echols comments, 'this view presupposes an innate and immutable maleness' (1984, p. 73). In that case, just what is the point of engaging in struggle against gender divisions at all? If it all boils down to some innate, essential quality, any attempt to change this state of affairs would be futile. In fact Raymond states that as sex reassignment surgery cannot change chromosomal sex, the transsexual does not really change sex at all. It would seem, then, that if chromosomes are the peg on which sexual divisions are hung we are left with scant possibility of any real change. The end product of Raymond's thesis is cultural feminism and a position which is, in Echol's words, 'committed to preserving rather than annihilating gender distinctions' (p. 66).

Carol Riddell is a post-operative transsexual, an active feminist and totally opposed to Raymond's analysis. She argues that the transsexual is unlikely to be a feminist because of the strictures imposed partly by society in general but particularly by the specialist medical profession, the 'empire' referred to by Raymond:

> Because of our biology, we were, usually, brought up as male children, forced to live as men in order to survive, and therefore developed ideas of what the actuality of women's existence is, that were seen through male identity blinkers. This distorted view was reinforced in many cases, by obligatory sexist counselling in order to get operations, and demands that we conform if we were to get an operation. (Riddell, 1980, p. 12).

Thus the male-to-female transsexual is unlikely in the first few years post-surgery to espouse a feminist approach to life, not only because of the expectations imposed by the medical profession, but because she has been subjected to masculine stereotypes of femininity for all of her life. If this is the case, what expectations can we have of transvestites? As biological men brought up within the confines of masculinity is it realistic to expect them to display a manifest desire to bring about the demise of patriarchy, the power of men? Most transvestites do not express any desire to become a woman in any permanent sense; their cross-dressing is a periodic activity, interspersed with work, social life and possibly marriage and fatherhood. Moreover, it is not just men who hold on to a tinsel notion of feminine stereotypes: many women do as well. Thus to single out a comparatively small number of men as some kind of revolutionary cadre is unrealistic.

How does this relate to transvestism? Unlike the transsexual, the transvestite does not attempt to change sex, or even to change gender appearance and behaviour, on a totally permanent basis. Now and then, with varying degrees of regularity, the transvestite crosses over the gender divide. The logical extension of Raymond's argument must be that the transvestite is a revolutionary in the battle against patriarchy because his actions confront and challenge the idea that men must be men. However, this does not come anywhere near to solving the dilemma posed by the case of transvestism. If we take Riddell's statement that 'it is not transsexualism which is the problem, but the way we are pressured to live in the world' (p. 15), and attempt to apply this to transvestism, we immediately run into problems. Neither the woman whose husband leaves her in order to become a woman himself, nor the woman who discovers her husband's love of dressing up in feminine clothing, is likely to swallow her emotions for the sake of the sexual revolution, or even social reform. And to offer this as a solution is no solution at all for those inadvertently caught up in it. It's one thing to claim, as Riddell does, that transvestism 'is clearly a product of patriarchal sex stereotypes' (p. 19), another entirely to expect it automatically to challenge those stereotypes.

Nevertheless, there are those who claim that cross-dressing does comprise some sort of attack on the gender role system and that it must, therefore, be viewed as a significant component of the struggle against this system. That transvestism upsets deeply held assumptions concerning the nature of femininity and masculinity cannot be denied, and thus arguments put forward for its potential as a vehicle for social change and liberation from the constriction of gender demarcation must be considered. Any challenge to male power immediately raises the question of gender roles and particularly the ways in which these are learned and internalised during childhood. While it has been stated that the transvestite switches gender roles, appearing for the most part as masculine, but at times feminine, another way of expressing this is to say that the transvestite lacks gender constancy. In other words, he does not necessarily see gender as an unvarying characteristic which never changes, despite alterations in appearance or behaviour. Given the restrictions of gender division we might ask if this is really such a bad thing. Surely an ability to see gender as fluid, ranging from the wholly 'masculine' to the wholly 'feminine', would help in destroying such division?

Transvestism and sexual politics

One way of looking at transvestism as a challenge to gender dichotomies is to place it in the context of androgyny – the combination of male and female which represents a more whole and complete self. This angle has been suggested by Talamini (1982) in a study of heterosexual transvestites. To demonstrate the historical and cross-cultural pervasiveness of the idea of androgyny and its association with the notion of wholeness, the complete being or self, Talamini draws upon a variety of religions: Taoism, Hinduism, Tantric Buddhism, Judaism and Christianity, along with shamanistic rituals, ancient Greek philosophy and the cultural practices of pre-industrial societies, and Jungian and modern psychology. The transvestite, he argues, is yet another facet of this drive towards perfection or completion of self: 'My view . . . is that cross-dressing is somehow bound up with the universal personal drive toward androgyny' (p. 66). This view comes close to the pro-transvestite literature, epitomised by Prince's claim that the transvestite represents human perfection. Unlike Prince, however, Talamini attempts to substantiate his claim using a sex role inventory scale (the BSRI). The scale comprises twenty masculine and twenty feminine characteristics, padded out with twenty neutral ones. In comparing the scores of two groups of heterosexual men matched for age and education, Talamini found that the transvestite group scored far higher on the measurement of androgyny than the non-transvestite group. This leads him to conclude that transvestism may be for many, if not all, transvestites a means of expressing an androgynous personality. 'As such, it may indicate a conception of mental health which is free from culturally imposed definitions of masculinity' (p. 70).

This is a weighty assertion and it is unfortunate that Talamini devotes so little space to it, because if it is the case that transvestites actually comprise the personification of androgyny, totality and the complete self – in short, the perfect human being – then surely the whole debate comes to a halt right here. It is not unreasonable to expect that most people would like to be able to feel themselves to be a whole person in their own right, and thus if transvestism can provide the pathway to achieving that end, if only for some, then it must, by definition, be accepted as a legitimate mode of expression of personhood, humanity and personal integrity. This is the angle on the complete self which also returns us to the debate concerning feminism and the role that men who transgress gender divisions may or may not play. Certainly it finds some expression in the views of transvestites themselves. Talamini quotes from an American transvestite publication, the *Journal of Male Feminism*, which insists that feminism devolves upon 'your right to be as feminine as your psyche directs'. On the basis of this somewhat unusual definition of feminism the editorial makes the claim for transvestism as a means towards psychic wholeness:

As feminists we claim the right to be whole human beings in public as well as in private, according to the psyches we have, not partial psyches cut back to fit old dominant-class biases. (quoted in Talamini, 1982, pp. 55–6)

Here, then, we find two, interrelated claims which, if accepted, would provide a new angle of vision on the question of sexual politics generally and the subjection of women specifically. First, the transvestite represents the unification of self, the complete human being, and is, by implication, superior to those who subscribe to culturally imposed, gender-related behaviour and attitudes. Second, despite his biological sex, the transvestite can also be a feminist precisely because he is able to express femininity as well as masculinity; he has the psyche of a feminist. This goes far beyond the claims made by Carol Riddell in her defence of the post-operative transsexual who identifies psychologically with feminism. What is being suggested here is that feminism is about self-expression, doing your own thing and combining as much femininity as you choose with a ready established masculinity.

Such repackaging of feminism is taken to further extremes in John Pepper's autobiography (1982). Pepper, a transvestite, documents his own personal history of cross-dressing from childhood to realisation that it enabled him to become 'more of a human being' (p. 82). He argues that the achievement of androgyny might well provide the ceasefire in the 'sex war' and thereby the inception of a truly human way of life:

> Even then I pondered however how wonderful it might be to be able, psychologically, to be both man and woman. What new light it could throw on everything we thought we knew. How much the sex war might be defused and happiness multiplied if we were no longer driven neurotically across the emotional battlefields of our lives – like the blind beasts of Flanders – to search for those lost, opposite halves of ourselves, tending always in the process to reduce human relationships to the pairings of cripples, not the many-faceted, truly creative unions of fully-grown people. (p. 75)

A passionate plea indeed for a more humanist way of relating and for a more wholistic, caring society; sentiments with which it would be churlish to disagree. But how does Pepper reach this conclusion and what does he see as the underlying problems which must be overcome if we are to move towards this androgynous utopia? In Pepper's scheme of things, women really have to do very little. Women, it seems, have choices, men are 'the underprivileged ones' (p. 84). A man is trapped, whilst a woman:

> could be a full-time mother *if she chose* or a careerist nowadays, or could stay at home to look after ageing parents if she had to, devote her life to 'good works' *or even ply as a prostitute*, all without too much trauma to her self-realization as a female. (p. 84, emphasis added)

So if men could be permitted freedom of sartorial expression, all our problems, at least in terms of gender division and sexism, will vanish. One could simply laugh this off and dismiss Pepper's obviously stereotyped and romanticised notions of femininity. After all, he did find that cross-dressing allowed him the treat of being in 'the high white tower . . . while some other bloody fool slew the dragons' (p. 83). But this goes beyond his failure to realise that women themselves have been struggling to get *out* of the tower that patriarchy built. If we remain at this point all we need to say is that Pepper is misguided in his analysis of both sexism and women's oppression and would be a lot better off forming a men's consciousness-raising group. But this takes us no further than Raymond's castigation of post-operative transsexuals. It's another way of saying that women, and only women, can engage in the struggle against sexism, that no man can possibly have any interest whatsoever in the demise of patriarchy and that any man who claims to be politically sympathetic to feminism is lying. In short, the only solution is separatism. For many women this is no solution at all, and for some men, at least, male power is something to be challenged.

Leaving aside the mistaken assumptions concerning feminism, femininity and the role of women in society, the claim that cross-dressing does provide a serious challenge to gender division must be considered. As outlined in Chapter 1, appearance is the outward and immediately visible indication of sex and gender, which are always assumed to fit together in the 'proper' way. Thus if this fit is upset does it not follow that the automatic correlation of sex with gender may begin to fall by the wayside and with it the constricting oppression of femininity and masculinity as polar and unequal opposites? As Kirk and Heath express it in their pictorial survey of varieties of cross-dressing, 'Are male stereotypes beginning to crumble, or is it just a case of "same meat, different gravy"?' (1984, p. 10). Is transvestism a means towards greater equality between the sexes and a breaking-down of the power politics of sex and gender, or is it another case of men retaining the privileges of masculinity?

The question arising here is, can there be anti-sexist cross-dressing? Do all transvestites engage with stereotyped notions of femininity of the sort that feminists have rejected, or are there alternatives which contribute towards the breaking-down of oppressive gender divisions? One means of opening up this debate is through the various non-commercial publications of transvestite organisations. More commonly though, they depict stereotypes of femininity which resist any possibility of attack on gender divisions. TV/TS produces its magazine *Glad Rag* six times a year, distributing it to all members. Its regular features include news of the new centre and current events; advice on buying clothes and underwear and applying make-up; articles on transvestites in history, transvestism and Christianity; fiction (such as a spoof on *The Wind in The Willows*, where Mole, Ratty and Toad are all transvestites); autobiographical experiences. These experiences tend to follow discernible patterns, whereby the transvestite is caught out by a wife or sister and is either told that he looks a mess and she helps him to improve his appearance or, alternatively, he meets with unexpected acceptance and approval. Some contrast has been provided by the inclusion of reports from the Partners' Support Group which, as outlined earlier, are sometimes directly critical. But the characteristic tenor of the magazine lies predominantly in its espousal of candyfloss-and-tinsel images of femininity.

More light is shed on the question of anti-sexist cross-dressing if we compare men dressing as women with women dressing as men. When women have impersonated men they have often adopted a somewhat androgynous image, especially on stage. Maitland's biography (1986) of the male impersonator, Vesta Tilley, emphasises this contrast. Whereas Vesta Tilley presented a flattering image of men, 'For a man to impersonate a woman is for him to undertake, voluntarily, an act of self-humiliation (unless he can make the woman sufficiently ridiculous for his identification with "her" to be seen as absurd)' (p. 89).

Why are male-to-female moves so much more shocking than female-to-male? Precisely because masculinity is accorded primacy, and thus a step down is, by definition, reprehensible. However, this line of argument does not entail the familiar cry of 'Poor men, they are so restricted by the confines of masculinity', because it is, after all, men who actively construct, protect and maintain the primacy of masculinity. Millett (1971) encapsulates this in her reference to the transvestite's enjoyment of the best of both worlds by becoming 'better than' a mere woman, because he is a 'woman' with a penis. The transgression of gender division is more apparent than real and does little to subvert the top ranking of masculinity and the gender divisions on which it is constructed. In effect, the transvestite simply bends the rules to his own satisfaction, periodically 'slumming it', but never relinquishing his claim to masculinity. The assertion that cross-dressing challenges gender divisions is lost on many transvestites. The majority dress in private simply to satisfy their own needs, not to join the vanguard of sexual revolution. Why such needs arise is unclear. Why a person becomes a transvestite can no more be explained than the process of becoming homosexual or heterosexual. All we can say is that it happens, and that the degree of censure commonly applied represents, in crystallised form, the demands made by patriarchal control for dichotomised gender wholly aligned with biological sex. Necessarily this censure is more harshly applied to men because they occupy primary status in the social ranking of gender. Transvestites exist, and will continue to do so, within a culture which defines masculinity as the norm, closely confined and totally distinct from femininity. The problem is that by seeing masculine and feminine as two entirely separate and exclusive entities, the transvestite's adoption of one persona automatically excludes the other. This produces fractured behaviour and can be an obstruction to human relations. In the words of a woman married to a transvestite:

> Cross-dressing seems to reinforce the sharp division of gender roles in the way in which it promotes stereotyped male and female ways of relating to other people. By separating their macho and gentle selves, transvestites are limiting their chances of being a balanced person and of balanced relationships between men and women. (Mitchell, 1987, p. 19).

Transvestism and marriage[1]

Those transvestites who attend group meetings and social functions are probably the tip of an iceberg; for every one who does become public, there are many more closeted in their own homes. Even less visible than this largely unknown group are the wives, often appearing as no more than shadowy figures attempting to cope with a problem. Of the transvestites discussed in Chapter 3, four had been married. Lucy and Yvonne claimed that their wives more or less tolerated their transvestism, although Lucy's wife stipulated that the neighbours should not find out. For both Anne and Candy there was hostility and an unwillingness or inability to accept the transvestite behaviour. Anne eventually left her wife after years of marriage in order to undergo sex reassignment surgery. Other married transvestites referred to their wives' dislike of their behaviour, but rarely elaborated, even when asked. It seemed that the women were largely invisible, overshadowed by the 'other women' in their men's lives. For the most part, they comprised an unknown quantity.

What did these wives experience during their marriage? Was there more than just the usual stress and strain associated with married life for these women? In fact, there are many unanswered questions here. How does a woman react to her husband's desire to wear women's clothing? More to the point, how does she feel when she only comes across this after years of marriage and raising a family? Does she decide to continue the relationship or end it, and if so, how? How does she cope with telling family and friends, or does it remain a deadly secret? And what is to be done about young children? The wife of a transvestite often faces problems like this alone, thinking that her problems are unique. She often blames herself. Maybe she isn't a good wife, doesn't provide the emotional and sexual satisfaction her husband needs. Or, if he really loved her, then surely he would give it up for her, or at least for the sake of the marriage and children.

Find the victim

In an American study, Deborah Feinbloom (1976) devotes some space to a consideration of transvestites' wives. Nevertheless, her subjects criticised her for paying insufficient attention to this largely unknown and important area. Posing the question 'Why do women stay married to transvestites?', she suggests three possibilities. First, that the woman suffers from low self-esteem. Thus she feels unable to find another man. She also feels that she may be the cause of his transvestism, possibly because she is insufficiently feminine herself. Second, she may really want a girlfriend in her husband. His transvestism, therefore, assuages the guilt surrounding her latent lesbian fantasies. Third, her life may be so dull and boring that her husband's behaviour may provide excitement and diversion from a humdrum existence.

Feinbloom suggests that a woman who stays married to a transvestite does so precisely because she herself suffers from some inadequacy or problem which she is unable to tackle directly or come to terms with. Her problem, then, is not simply that her man is a transvestite, but rather that it has highlighted and brought to the fore problems in herself. However, we do not know if it is really possible that a wife may reach such a level of tolerance that her husband's transvestism presents no more difficulties for her than the fact that he always leaves the cap off the toothpaste. Not only is such acceptance likely to be hidden but one of the specific difficulties here is that Feinbloom is looking at women in the context of someone else's information. A wife's situation, feelings, conflicts and anger cannot be conveyed through an analysis which is derived second-hand or imposed from the outside. A woman may accept her husband's behaviour because her life is so dull, but that is true of many women's lives. Similarly, lack of self-esteem or lesbian fantasies are hardly peculiar to the wife of a transvestite. Such characteristics may be fairly common; but Feinbloom presents them as 'explanations', when in reality we have not progressed beyond the level of 'chicken and egg' speculation.

In a similar vein, Steiner (1985) comments that women who live with transvestite men usually suffer from poor self-image and do not see themselves as attractive or desirable. What she fails to explain, however, is whether these feelings emerged prior to or following the discovery of the man's transvestism. In other words, does a woman stay with a transvestite because she has a low opinion of herself, or does her self-image emanate from her knowledge of his behaviour?

Indeed this line of inquiry can run onto dangerous ground; a point which has been debated in greater depth in relation to abusive marriages. Why does a woman stay with a violent husband, or, having left him, return to him? Time and time again it has been suggested that these women are somehow 'different', that they 'enjoy' the excitement and the tension, the rush of adrenalin, if not the actual beatings. Alternatively, or even coincidentally, they are emotionally inadequate flirts, man-haters who will taunt a man relentlessly until he, understandably, loses control. So the blame is partially the woman's – she has nagged, failed in her 'proper' role of wife and mother and thereby contributed to the outbursts of violence. Not surprisingly she too begins to wonder if she is at fault.

From the outside it may appear illogical and even masochistic to remain with a violent man, but once the women are given the opportunity to tell their own stories, to place the facts in context, a different picture emerges.[2] Primary concerns are children and money; where to go, how to cope with children, how to uproot them from home, school and friends, how to finance this. Equally there is fear, the need to find a place of safety; and often there is hope – that this time the man she loved and married will keep his promise not to beat her again. When considered from the woman's point of view, it becomes understandable why she stayed so long or why she agreed to give him yet another chance.

Blaming the victim

Blaming the victim takes several forms, from a direct attack on behaviour which, it is claimed, was a precipitating factor, to refusing to acknowledge that there is a victim at all. West (1974), for instance, subscribes to J. S. Mill's dictum that restraint should only be imposed if an activity harms others, adding that the burden of proof should lie with those who seek to prohibit. But how do we define harm? The transvestite may not be harming his wife in any physical sense; nevertheless, 'although they [transvestites] argue their activities do no harm to anyone, many of the wives can be seen as carrying a considerable psychological burden'.[3] The stress experienced by some wives is illustrated in the following chapter.

There are other, more subtle forms of blaming the victim which, while not directly making accusations of precipitation, still suggest that she could have avoided the situation and is, therefore, complicit in some way. There is the battered wife who 'self-selects' from one violent situation to the next; the rape victim who is 'more likely' to be attacked. Thus, some of the heat is taken off the violent husband or the rapist; though he did it, *she* must shoulder the blame. When such attitudes infiltrate academic research they are invested with a certain amount of authority, even more so when reproduced by those of renown and academic standing.

In the treatment of sexual deviance, women can be quite useful.

For example, a measure of success during therapy with a male homosexual has been linked to his achieving intercourse with a woman – not a particular woman, just any woman, a useful receptacle.[4] Women are also significant in their roles as wives and homemakers. A programme of psychotherapy was conducted with the wives of sexual deviants (paedophiliacs, exhibitionists and obscene phone-callers), not because the wives themselves necessarily needed or requested it, but because it was felt that a change in the wife's approach would help induce a change in the husband![5] Of the women receiving therapy only three are reported in detail. All had experienced emotionally unstable childhoods, and, although aware of their husbands' activities, had maintained a conspiracy of silence, pretending it wasn't happening and thereby, it is claimed, perpetuating the deviance. From this it is deduced that the women derived psychological gain from their husband's behaviour, specifically some sort of vicarious satisfaction of their own feelings of hostility towards women. That may be so, but what is abundantly clear is the extent to which each woman played out in extreme form the wifely role. One was supportive of her husband and stood by him throughout. One had sex with him when she did not want to in an attempt to prevent another deviant episode. Another woman even shaved off her pubic hair in the hope that this would arrest her husband's paedophilia. They tried to avoid public disgrace, private confrontation and personal upheaval. But how much choice did these women really have? Given all the problems there are in leaving a husband, are they to be blamed for staying? And, more important, does the type of support they gave render them mentally, emotionally and sexually deficient?

This type of 'heads I win, tails you lose' approach is amply demonstrated by research carried out with eighteen wives of transvestites at Johns Hopkins Hospital.[6] The marriages ranged in duration from one to 35 years. Only five of the women had known about their husbands' transvestism prior to marriage. Seven were diagnosed as suffering from depressive neuroses, one from anorexia nervosa, while the remaining ten 'had no clear psychiatric diagnosis' – which presumably means there was nothing wrong with them. Nevertheless, it is stated that the women's reactions ranged from hysterical repression or denial to passive-dependent coping strategies. So, angry or resigned, these women became problems in themselves as a result of remaining with a transvestite husband despite the fact that they disliked his behaviour. Two women had discovered female clothing in their husband's drawer and assumed that he was having an affair with another woman. This is interpreted as an hysterical defence, a form of repression and denial of reality, even though the assumption may have been the most logical initially. As a result of staying with their husbands all the women sacrificed their self-esteem, and thus they are labelled 'moral masochists', people who derive psychological gain from suffering. The implication here is that some sort of choice or self-selection is involved. Although some of the women only found out about their husbands' transvestism after years of marriage and having families to care for, it is suggested that their early childhood experiences 'propelled' them into marriage with these men.

On the one hand, the wife who stays with her deviant husband for the sake of the children, lack of alternatives, or even her love for him, is almost, by definition, psychologically deficient. On the other, the wife who leaves her husband because of his deviance is also lacking because it was her own inadequacies which impelled her to marry him in the first place. These wives are trapped in the position of the fictitious child who, on being asked by a police officer why he was running round and round the block, explains that he is running away from home, but his father will not allow him to cross the road.

In an examination of the effects of transvestism on women, Robert Stoller both inverts and expands the entire issue, claiming that women, as mothers, sisters, girlfriends and wives, actually cause and maintain it. The first cause is woman: a mother or a sister seeking power and control over the man. She may be 'a forceful leader of ladies' clubs, another a crabbed masochist, a third a tired, graceful, faceless housewife, a fourth, though not clinically psychotic, has truly believed since childhood that she is a witch . . . ' (1967, p. 333). Stoller projects three analytic categories onto women in an attempt to codify some of the different ways in which women initiate and maintain transvestite behaviour. The 'malicious man-hater' will humiliate a male at any opportunity. Her anger and her need for revenge on men so damages the male child's gender identity that his means of coping with and fending off such domination is through cross-dressing. In contrast 'the succourer' does not actually cause transvestism, rather she will support its already established existence. She is the woman who, having married a transvestite, adjusts easily. The third type is 'the symbiote' whose underlying depression and hostility to men is expressed through her inability to allow her infant son normal separation from her, thereby causing his later transsexualism. Stoller admits that his typology is not exhaustive, but the outstanding feature is still the hatred of men expressed by the women supposedly responsible for the cause and continuation of transvestism. The wife who attempts to support and care for her husband is denigrated as a 'succourer', while he becomes the passive victim of both her and a male-hating, female relative. But why do some women hate men? Must it all be 'explained' by the infinite regression into parent/child psychodynamics? Is the transvestite so utterly blameless that a wife must simply accept that he became a transvestite because of the women in his life?

In this way of thinking, the transvestite does not cause the psychological stress for the wife; instead the situation is reversed. The wives are acting out their own psychological problems, and thus are in need of treatment so that they may adjust to their husbands' needs. Or, if they have already adjusted, this too is the outcome of some personalised, psychosexual orientation. But what is the wife attempting to adjust to, what precisely does she have to come to terms with being married to a transvestite? If he is, in all other respects, a good husband and father, does the fact that he periodically engages in gender-inappropriate behaviour or sexual fetishism really comprise serious difficulties?

Marriage to a transvestite

For a wife, marriage to a transvestite can entail aspects of the eternal triangle, because while there is not another woman in the literal sense of the term, figuratively there is. The husband is cross-dressing for sexual pleasure, bringing a personal reality to his fantasy of the ideal woman. In other words, the husband becomes 'the other woman'. So while the wife may adopt a brave front and pretence of acceptance, privately she may be extremely unhappy about it. As Benjamin has pointed out, 'The husband's ability as a lover and the wife's sexual needs are often deciding factors as to whether a marriage can endure or not. Some can . . . many cannot' (1966, p. 44).

In some cases the husband will need objects or 'props' if he is to enjoy sex with his wife. These props will take the form of clothing (as opposed to the trappings of bondage or sado-masochism, for example). Not surprisingly, from her point of view this creates a barrier between them. Prince and Bentler (1972) surveyed 500 transvestites, over 90 per cent of whom claimed to be heterosexual. More than a quarter of them liked to wear a nightie during sex and 20 per cent liked 'full costume'. Unfortunately we have no way of knowing how the wives felt about making love like this.

In addition to the apparent fetishism which her husband may introduce into their sexual relationship, a wife will commonly experience anxieties which are difficult to deal with. Is she sexually inadequate and is it because of her shortcomings that he periodically feels the need to become a woman himself? Is he really homosexual and likely to have affairs with other men when he is dressed as a woman? If she tried to understand his needs, would he perhaps take it much further and want to dress all the time, and even perhaps decide that he wants to become a woman physically as well? Will this have a damaging effect on the children if they see their father cross-dressed; or, indeed, is it an hereditary disease? Typically, a wife will be beset by some or all of these fears. While some writers claim that there is no basis for them, there are married transvestites who have affairs with men or who eventually decide to opt for sex reassignment surgery. Moreover, there can be few women who are so confident and secure in their own sexuality that they do not feel threatened when faced with a problem of this nature.

Another major question relates to the sexual aspect of transvestism. Is it primarily a sexual perversion associated with clothes fetishism, or is it more a case of gender motivation with sexuality playing no more than an incidental role? Opinions vary tremendously here. Some writers emphatically deny the sexual orientation; others see it as a transitory phase; still others argue that the primary focus is indeed a sexual one. Such disparity is mirrored by the responses of transvestites' wives. Some complain about their husbands masturbating or wanting to have sex with them while cross-dressed; others say that it is simply a means of relaxation and that sex is an irrelevant factor or something which belongs to the past. Transvestites often insist that although sexual gratification may be paramount during teenage years or early twenties, the transvestite does mature out of this stage and continues to dress simply for relaxation and relief from the oppressive strains of masculinity.

On the grounds that pornography directed to the transvestite tends towards auto-eroticism only, Ackroyd (1979) argues that exclusive sexualisation of transvestism is an overblown distortion of its reality. Presumably Ackroyd does not consider self-stimulation to be sexual. More realistically perhaps, Benjamin recognises what he calls the 'sexual overtones' of a behavioural problem, stating that 'to take sex out of transvestism is like taking music out of opera' (1966, p. 37). In making this point he stands in direct opposition to Prince (1967), who insists that cross-dressing functions to fulfil and express the feminine elements of the masculine personality and is, therefore, the completion of gender and quite unrelated to sex. As the prime mover for FPE, the Foundation for Full Personality Expression (an American organisation catering to heterosexual transvestites), Prince has clearly vested interests. How much easier it is to promote a supposedly sexually deviant form of behaviour as non-perverted and harmless when it is sanitised for public consumption.

In terms of the literature dealing with transvestism there are, on balance, more writers who would see it as sexual than not, largely as a result of their leanings towards psychoanalytic theory. If cross-dressing is viewed as some sort of defence emanating from unresolved childhood trauma associated with the fear of castration, then naturally it will be seen as a mainly sexual phenomenon. Female clothing, particularly of the more sensuous kind, is considered to be a substitute for interpersonal sex, and the transvestite himself becomes the surrogate female, the 'phallic woman'.[7] But if this is so, why do some desire heterosexual relations aided not by the woman wearing the frilly nightie or the sexy underwear, but by wearing it themselves? If it is for the purpose of allaying castration fears, then why does this function become redundant for some men and not for others? The meaning assigned to cross-dressing varies from one transvestite to another, yet psychiatrists, psychologists and psychoanalysts have consistently attempted to pin on to it a single cause, asserting that it is, in all cases, either primarily sexual or not sexual at all. From the standpoint of a woman married to a transvestite man, this whole debate may well seem academic and irrelevant. In this respect, we will understand more from considering the wives' own stories and experiences.

6

Wives talking

Whatever the cause, transvestism will undoubtedly exert some effect on a marital relationship. It is rare that a wife will actively and unreservedly enjoy her husband's transvestism despite the dictate of 'accept and enjoy' propounded in some of the pro-transvestite literature. Certainly those who come to terms with it have suffered periods of distress. The suggestion that such distress reflects inadequacy or emotional immaturity in the woman herself finds no basis in women's own accounts of their experiences. Initial reactions tend towards shock and disgust, and of those who have reached some level of understanding, none of the wives whose stories are reproduced here felt able to treat her husband's transvestism with complete equanimity.

Of course, these women may not be typical wives of transvestites; it could be that they have experienced more difficulty than most. For each woman who has reacted against it strongly there may be many more who happily accept their husband's transvestism; but I suspect not. Meetings of the Partners' Support Group at TV/TS focused on the difficulties wives faced, and although there were a few women who were accepting, they had not always felt like that. As for those who divorce their husband because of his transvestism, they remain an unknown quantity.

Any attempt to uncover women's reactions and feelings about transvestism by asking their men will most probably result in second-hand, distorted views.[1] With this in mind I visited women in their own homes and interviewed them alone for several hours. The five women depicted here were contacted through the Transvestite/ Transsexual Support Group, and Women of the Beaumont Society

(WOBS), an informal group set up by and for wives of transvestites. In many respects this proved to be the most difficult area to research because it involved making contact with an invisible population. During the six months of fieldwork at TV/TS, three wives visited once, and only one returned (although this has now changed with the establishment of the partners' support group). Any discussion was hampered by the confines of the room and the proximity of the woman's husband and his friends. Obviously they could not feel at ease discussing personal problems in such a setting. Nevertheless, it became increasingly clear that wives experience difficulties with their husbands' transvestism and that this is an area where investigation is long overdue.

The interviews covered several main areas: biographical information, the initial discovery of the husband's transvestism, reactions and methods of coping, and dealing with children, family and friends. Overall the women told their own stories with minimal interruption. The names have been changed and each woman has chosen a name for herself and her husband, with the exception of Polly who because of her public campaigning was happy to be identified. All the wives have given permission for the interviews to be reproduced, and personal details of occupations or life events which could identify them have been altered or omitted altogether. The stories have been grouped in the following way. First we look at Eleanor and June, both of whom found out about their husbands' transvestism after years of marriage and raising a family. After a long period of intense difficulty both have reached a point where they have come to terms with the situation, although they still have reservations. One of the problems in attempting to assess the effect of transvestism in marriage is that possibly there will already be some problems which have not been resolved and are brought to the surface when the transvestism is discovered. For both Eleanor and June their marriages came close to breaking point, but have survived largely because of compromises made by both partners. Polly experienced less difficulty in dealing with her husband's transvestism and has taken her acceptance outside of the home by helping other wives. Susan and Leonie do not see a clear way forward and so have not ruled out divorce, but they are still hopeful that things will change for the better.

Eleanor

Eleanor is 44 and has been married to Will for twenty-five years.
They have three children, two of them married: the youngest is 18
and lives at home. Eleanor works as a cashier; Will is a maintenance
supervisor. He told Eleanor about his transvestism three years ago.
She described this:

One day I went up to the bathroom, and at the back of the
cupboard we've got up there, there was a girdle, and I thought,
'Well that's strange, what's that doing there?' And he said he was
wearing it because he was getting paunchy and he wanted to pull it
in. I just said, 'Well, as long as you don't wear it out in the street, I
don't care', but I never gave it any more thought than that.

One day he started talking about it and he said that he liked to
dress in women's clothes. I just said 'Oh' and left it at that and
went and did something else. Then he had a day off from work
and he rang me up at work and asked me if I was coming home at
lunchtime. Then he said he was going to be dressed. I came in and
he was sitting in the kitchen and I just looked at him. His clothes
didn't match, his make-up was awful. He made me feel sick, he
looked so hideous that I didn't know whether to laugh or cry. I
couldn't say anything, I was just numb. I drank my coffee, ate my
sandwich, got up and walked out. I went back to work and rang
him up in the afternoon and he'd obviously had some drink, and
he said, 'This is what I've got to do, and you've just got to accept
it.'

Three thoughts went through my head: he was gay, there was
something wrong with me, or there was another woman. Well, I
thought, the other woman's out. I mean we weren't great
party-goers, there was no fear of him flirting with anyone else. So
I thought he was gay or there was something wrong with me.
After all these years, all of a sudden I didn't satisfy him sexually. I
suppose I'm not an over-sexed person, I suppose I'm quite
normal, but I don't know what normal is.

I said to him, 'Well, is there something wrong with me? Don't I
give you what you want out of our marriage that you feel you'd
rather be a woman than a man?' And he said he still loved me, but
I said 'You can't if you want to do all this.' In the end we just
didn't talk to each other. For six, seven months we were here, we

didn't go out with each other, we didn't talk to each other, and it was just hell really. If it hadn't been for Tracy I would have just packed my bags and gone.

I had just started working full-time again, so I was in a position to buy clothes and I didn't have to think about the children. When I bought something he'd say, 'I don't like that. What do you want that for? You've got plenty of stuff upstairs, you don't want that.' I got to the stage I was buying something, hiding it in the wardrobe and then wearing it. And he's saying, 'That's new,' and I'm saying, 'I've had it for ages.' I got really sneaky about things because it just caused an argument every time I bought anything. Now I think about it, obviously it was because everything he was getting was from jumble sales.

The initial discovery of Will's transvestism had repercussions which went far beyond the immediate situation. Eleanor felt that their long-standing marriage was under threat and she began to rethink their relationship and their life together. Gradually events and activities of the past took on new meaning as Eleanor increasingly saw her husband primarily as a man who wanted to dress up as a woman. She realised that his absorption in various hobbies over the years had been a way of sublimating his transvestism, that he had managed to push it to one side, but now he had started cross-dressing again:

I thought maybe now he'd want to go all the way and become a woman, and then I would have nothing, you know. I suppose I was trying to hold on to my life really, because I'd been married twenty-two years.

Sometimes he would say, 'Can I dress?', and I would sit there and think 'Oh, don't be mean, let him do it.' But as soon as he came down here I would clam up. We wouldn't talk to each other because I didn't really want to talk to him, sitting there looking like that. He didn't look so hideous then because I sort of tried to calm him down a bit. I said, 'Right, if I've got to sit and look at you, you've got to look reasonable.' I mean, when you see all these drag artists on television, it's all over the top, isn't it? They don't look like ordinary, everyday women, do they?'

Eleanor still finds this lack of realism and attachment to fantasy a problem. More than this, she found the sexual aspects of Will's transvestism particularly difficult; in order to deal with this, she has established certain ground-rules:

I wouldn't let him go to bed in a nightdress, or his make-up or anything. I said, 'If you want to wear a nightdress, there's a spare bed in there.' Well, I wouldn't dream of going to bed with another woman, and that's what he wanted to be, wasn't it? It was the image, it was the make-up and hair. I didn't see him as Will – no, I don't think that's right actually. I did see him as Will, Will underneath, but it wasn't like him. I don't like him holding my hand or touching me when he's dressed. It just makes me go cold. He does feel very sexy after he's dressed; I think he would feel more sexy if he could wear his nightie, but I don't see why they've got to go to bed with nightdresses and wigs and make-up.

Their relationship deteriorated to the point where it seemed that the marriage might end. Besides dealing with her own feelings, Eleanor was also concerned about their children, particularly Tracy who still lives at home:

When he dressed at home I was tensed up all the time because we don't lock doors here and what if the kids just walked in the door and he's sitting there? I suppose I was trying to protect them really. I didn't want them to know their father dressed in women's clothes. Will said we had to tell Tracy because she was going through a funny stage, she was getting moody and we couldn't understand why. That was two years ago when she was 16. So he took her to one side and told her, and she said, 'Oh, I already know.' We said, 'Well, why didn't you tell us?' She said, 'Well, you didn't want me to know so I didn't say anything to you.' Tracy found the clothes in the wardrobe. She had told Sandra, my eldest, and Sandra had said, 'Well, it's his thing.' But Tracy's seen him dressed a few times and I can see the change in her when he's dressed. Alright, she laughs and jokes with him, but it's all a front.
  I don't even know how I stayed sane. I didn't tell anyone, you see. To me, it was so outrageous, I couldn't tell anybody. I suppose we were lucky that we went to TV/TS as early on as we did. Maybe if it had gone on a little bit longer, I'd have found I

couldn't cope with it, because I think I was on the verge of having a breakdown actually. Really, if it hadn't been for Yvonne [Sinclair], to have someone to talk to, I think I would have gone mad.

Eleanor and Will have survived the crisis in their marriage by compromise and give-and-take on both sides. This has even been beneficial in the sense that Eleanor feels that their marriage is now much stronger:

I think it was gradual – getting back together. It didn't suddenly go click, everything's OK now. For the first year to eighteen months, we had to go to TV/TS every weekend, we *had* to go. But then he got to the period where he would say, 'Oh well, we won't go this week, I don't need to go this week.' And so, sort of slowly I suppose, we built up our lives again. He's felt more secure, and that, I suppose, rubs off on me really, to know that he's happier now.

With a bit of luck it might fade away. I don't feel as bad as I did, because I've come to accept it more. I don't like it; I just hope that it'll go away and he just won't want to do it, but I don't think it will ever come to that point, quite honestly. I think it's always going to be there and it's something I've got to accept. If someone could give me a reason why they want to do it I'd feel a lot better. But I mean, it's three years now, but I still don't understand why – and nobody can tell me why.

I suppose I have given a lot, and Will has given a lot. I mean he could say, 'Right, this is something I want to do and I'm going to do it every single night of the week.' I go to TV/TS with him because I know that it's one way of getting it out of his system for a week. All the same, if Will said he'd give it up tomorrow and never do it again, I'd give up smoking – and *that* would be hard!

June

June is 38 and works part-time in a factory. She has been married to George, a gas-fitter, for twenty-one years. They have two teenage children, both still at school, and they live in a small house in a town in south-east England. Eight years ago, George told June that he had been a transvestite since he was a teenager. This acted as a catalyst, bringing problems which already existed to a head. It has taken them until recently to reach a solution:

Three months before he told me I was already very depressed, very nervous. I detected that something was wrong with George, but he wouldn't tell me what it was; all I knew was that he'd cut himself off, he'd put barriers up. He wasn't cruel or nasty to me, but he would just eat his food when it was put in front of him and he'd read his book, and that was it. I couldn't cope with life and I had to have tranquillisers. I was put on all these tablets, Librium and anti-depressants, which lifted me up – I felt ever so good, you know. We were walking round the shops one day and we stopped at a clothes shop. Suddenly George put his arms round me and told me how much he loved dresses as well. He thought I was alright, but it was the Librium that was making me high.

June spent the next three months trying to come to terms with George's confession, but her depression made it more difficult for her to cope with any additional problems and she became increasingly anxious:

First of all when he told me, I let him have the go-ahead and he could dress. The children were a lot younger then, so when they'd gone to bed, he could come down dressed; but then something inside you rebels and is repulsed and says, 'This isn't right.' You married a man and you've got this man dressing as a woman and enjoying the role. I just cracked up and kept crying. And it was more and more tablets.

Oh, I had a lot to be angry about, a lot to be bitter about. Of course, when he could have the go-ahead, all these things came down from the loft. All these wigs appeared and all this underwear – looking at my dressing-table it was just like another woman had come in and taken over. I thought, 'My God, there's me scrimping and saving on the housekeeping, and things I went without, and there's all this.'

Once he got the go-ahead, he wanted to dress every night. And, I mean, he was totally relaxed and at peace, he was really lovely to live with. I mean, he was ever so helpful, whereas before he wouldn't do a thing. And he'd help me with the washing-up and he'd help me in the house, whereas before I just had to do the lot. I remember a couple of nights I let him wear a nightie, but something inside says no, it's just not on. Once he wanted to make love like it, and I let him, but I think that just shattered me. I couldn't even discuss it. I couldn't talk about it – we just swept it under the carpet and I ended up in the local psychiatric hospital.

Not only did June have psychiatric treatment but the prescriptions for the anti-depressants continued. Consequently she became dependant:

The hospital just thought it was me, little old housewife, couldn't cope with life – anxiety neurosis, I think it was called. I got depressed and cried a lot, so they just gave me more and more tablets and ECT as well. I did a very good cover-up job to get out, making out I was alright.

I'd been going to church on and off, because a couple of people I knew that were very insecure like me – their husbands died – they suddenly found God and were able to cope with life. And I thought, 'Well, if it can happen to them, it can happen to me', but I just couldn't see the light.

I tried to come off the tablets, I went three days without any – three days and three nights – and terrible withdrawal symptoms. It was absolutely horrific – I just can't describe it, I thought I was going absolutely insane. I was aiming for the door and hitting the wall. I was in a terrible state. It was about half past three in the morning and George was snoring his head off. I just felt so exhausted and weak, I thought, 'I just don't know how to cope with this – me, my nerves, transvestite problems.' And I was ready to take my tablets, I had them all in a little bottle, I was ready to take them all, to end my life.

I prayed, 'Oh Lord, help me to help myself.' And as I said it, I thought the bedroom had lit up. But it wasn't the bedroom, it was my mind. It took ages for my mind to take in what I was experiencing. I couldn't see Jesus in flesh and blood but there was this presence. It was so strong, so beautiful – a love that is pure. He's got a terrific sense of humour too, because my first reaction was, 'Oh, I've got my rollers in.' But it didn't matter, he loved me just as I am. All the things that I told him I was frightened of, what was wrong, really it was faults within me and I hadn't recognised it. It was as if he was just taking it, throwing it over his shoulder and just giving me love.

For two weeks June was, in her words, 'on a spiritual high', but then she went back to her previous state. She was helped by the minister of her church who arranged for her to stay at a convalescent home run by the church. She spent eight months there:

It's taken me all this time to work through, to get a lot of that anger and jealousy and resentment out. I was taking a lot out on George – blaming him, his transvestite problem – when really I was very insecure, very immature in coping with anything really. I don't blame George at all now, but I did then. You know he says, 'Oh God made me like this', but I still can't believe that God would make him like that. I'm sure it's something that has happened in his childhood. It could be a way of escaping – you know, escapism into the female role, wanting protection. They think that women have a better life than men, but it's totally untrue. You can't escape from pain and problems, can you? You've still got to face up to them whether you wear a skirt or trousers.

He dresses about once a month now. Sometimes all the hairs have to come off his legs, and that is one thing I don't like because that's what attracts. Dressed up as a woman he doesn't turn me on at all. He knows he doesn't turn me on. He knows that I prefer him as a man. But it doesn't affect me like it used to. I do get tense, but then it dies down. I think, 'Well, it's only going to be for a few hours and then he's going to get changed.' The more relaxed I am, the more relaxed he's becoming and his need to dress isn't so frequent.

Well, I've come this far and I'm not going to go back. I'm determined to see it through. I mean, there's no cure as such, but I don't think any woman can totally accept it. I couldn't stand it if my children found out. His wigs and clothes are in my wardrobe, so the boys don't know. George doesn't leave his make-up out, he's got that in a drawer – but the boys would think it was mine.

I'm sure it will be something that will gradually get less and less. I mean, when George is an old man, he can't go and get his pension, toddling down the road, us arm-in-arm, him with a dress on and a wig! He can't deny himself as a man, you see.

Polly

Polly is 36. She and Ron lived together for three years before getting married six years ago. They have four children from Polly's previous marriage. Ron has his own construction business; Polly runs the office administration from home. 'I've been a mother and a housewife from the year dot,' she says. She is the local organiser of WOBS, Women of the Beaumont Society, which she set up in 1981 to help women whose partners are transvestites. Unlike the other women featured here, Polly is accustomed to talking about transvestism. She often talks to other wives, has been interviewed on television and featured in a national newspaper. She described her discovery of Ron's transvestism:

It happened just when he moved in with me. The baby was crying, and he went in to her. It was freezing cold and he asked if he could put my nightdress on. I didn't really take any notice of it. I said 'Don't make a habit of it', and that was it. A few days later, quite by chance, I picked up a magazine and it had an article about transvestism. I said to him, 'Are you a transvestite?' And of course the whole defence mechanism went into action and he denied it.

At first, Polly's reaction was that it was nothing to worry about, and as the relationship was new, she was even more willing to go along with Ron's dressing:

At first, I couldn't see anything odd in it at all, because I dressed as I wanted to – jeans or dress, I couldn't see what the big hang-up was. Obviously I realise it now, but at the time it seemed very cut-and-dried. So he puts on a dress occasionally, what's that to me? It's when you learn you get a change of personality at times as well, then it starts to worry you. I'm sure if you've just moved in with somebody, they could tell you they were a mass-murderer, you wouldn't give a damn.

After her initial acceptance Polly now began to feel that she was less able to cope and that Ron's transvestism was getting out of proportion:

I thought that the more open we were about it the less important it would be. In fact, it did the reverse and that's when I felt threatened. I felt it had completely taken over, he didn't need me any more. All he had to do was dress and he'd escaped into this other world. I felt totally rejected, unable to cope, I felt that it completely dominated my life. But I didn't know how to stop it without going against all what I'd said, that was the hard part.

What happened was he became more and more relaxed and more and more able to dress, and he lost his identity somewhere. He was almost convinced that he shouldn't have been a man at all. The only thing that kept me going was the fact that he wasn't gay.

Then I said I didn't want him to dress as often, so he stopped. Consequently that made him uptight, miserable, and he got a chip on his shoulder, as though he suddenly wasn't good enough for me – and that annoyed me even more. It made us distant enough to start using it as an excuse. I think it was probably because we'd moved in together almost as soon as meeting each other, so it was just inevitable that a break would come, be it over transvestism or anything else. We separated for about three months. It was in those three months that I decided I had to find out as much as I could – what was needed – and actually all that was needed was somebody else in the same position.

I spoke to Marriage Guidance and they didn't really know what I was talking about. But they got in touch with the Beaumont Society who put someone in touch with us. When Ron realised that there were quite a few other people like this, he began to settle down. The Beaumont Society offered contact and the opportunity to get out of the house, away from where I thought it would harm the children.

It's a very self-orientated thing, it's like turning yourself into what you want. They want the partner to be dominant, and that's what the woman can't cope with. I think they can cope with the dressing and even the sex while dressed, but it's this having to play the man while he's being feminine. If it was sex for Ron, he would only dress for sex. Before I knew it wasn't for sex, I did lead it that way to find out for my own curiosity. It did nothing for him, which was fortunate because it did nothing for me either! I think a good word instead of 'sexual' would be 'sensual'.

I don't feel threatened. The only thing I feel threatened by – and it sounds silly to say it – is what they get out of it. It does annoy me – the posing – because if I do my fingernails I know within probably a couple of hours they'll be chipped. I don't like being up to my eyes in washing-up, but that's part of the job, it sort of comes with being a mum more than anything else. So it does annoy me when he can sit there and pose. It's a false image, a complete fantasy. I feel in control of the situation now. Where women fall flat on their face, the same as I can sometimes, is when you feel out of control. When it was all touch-and-go, my way round things was to try to prove I didn't mind. I don't know who I was trying to prove it to, mind you – probably to me. I actually said to him, 'You can shave your legs to look decent when we go out.' It took about three years to pluck up the courage to reverse that decision but I got round it by coinciding it with pierced ears, which you can see when he's male. I just turned round in the kitchen one day and said, 'You can have your ears pierced', after thinking about if for six months. But when he came home, I made a fuss about how nice the earrings were, and I said, 'I wish you wouldn't shave your legs.' He immediately said, 'Why not?' I said, 'Because men are hairy. It's taken a bit more of the man than I want.' I know he would like to, but he doesn't, purely for my feelings.

Logic tells me that if you choose to do something you can choose not to do something. That's what makes it so hard to cope with, because it's an uncontrollable and incurable thing. Most of the time they don't want it controlled or cured anyway, so you know you can't win. It's a battle that you're never going to win, and you've got to come to terms with the fact that you've got to come second. I mean, I am fully aware that my husband will step out in front of a bus and save me from sudden death, but I also know that if the actual choice were, 'I can never dress again', there would be a moment's hesitation and I would be gone. If transvestites are wise – and many are, of course – they make a woman feel so needed and feminine the rest of the time that it compensates.

The children are aware of Ron's transvestism. They have either been told about it by Polly or they have found out for themselves:

Originally I worried about the effect it would have on the kids. It all came about mainly because I was forced into it. The oldest one, who was about 14, started to ask me questions. Thinking back – and I laugh about it now – it's stupid the things you do not to be found out! In fact you're making it obvious that something's wrong. I'd barricade the door with my body if they went to leave the room when he was dressed and about to leave the house. And they kept saying, 'Why? What's going on out there?' I thought it was better for them to know than to wonder, and when we told the oldest one, his only statement about it was, 'Is that all?' His mind had worked out something pretty awful and made it a lot worse than it actually was. Anyway, he then told his brother.

The third one actually did find out: he walked in, quite by chance, and he couldn't keep a straight face. He laughed, then forced his face in a straight line and said, 'I really don't care', and went out again and that was it. He's never bothered since.

Then it was going on television that did it. When I did the interview, Joanne told her teacher who, fortunately said, 'Oh well, if that's what your mummy believes, she should do it. Good for her.' As regards her school friends, she said to them that she'd been to the studios. They said, 'Why was your mummy there?' So she said, 'You wouldn't understand if I told you.' She feels they wouldn't have understood, so there was no point in telling them, which was a fair assumption for such a little head to work out.

I've never said they mustn't tell; I've left it completely up to them. They know how society reacts, it's up to them if they want other people to know about themselves. I mean, they never had a dad in a dress wandering about doing the house-work. It's always been Mum and Dad. Even when he's dressed, it's Dad. They've no hang-ups about that at all, no doubts.

Polly spends much of her spare time helping other women married to transvestites, which also satisfies her need to talk to someone in a similar position. She initiated a wives' group which meets to discuss problems and has produced a pamphlet for women in the same situation. One unexpected result of 'going public' is that it is often assumed that Polly is completely pro-transvestism and able to accept it without reservation:

When we had the first WOBS meetings we were adamant that there must not be any husbands there, because we couldn't say

what we wanted to. We'd all have different walks of life, but all
the way through our feelings about transvestism were the same
and that was very heartening for us. Because women do have an
awful guilt complex about it being their fault. Even when you've
explained that it was there before they met him, they still feel they
must be lacking.

I don't think women lack understanding, I think what they
don't understand is their own attitude. I don't know why I get
worried or uptight about the situation, because when I think
about it, what is there to get uptight about? What is so difficult
about just seeing someone in a dress occasionally? But it doesn't
matter how much I convince myself or others that this is alright,
its not alright. Otherwise I wouldn't mind at all, but I don't know
what's wrong with it. That's the trouble – I don't actually know
why I feel like I do. I get very annoyed that transvestites can stick
one item of clothing on and feel so totally relaxed, while I can still
feel all wound up – I don't know how it's being done.

Some men hit the bottle, then their wives. I suppose out of the
two, this is much better. But some wives – they almost see
drinking as the better option, because something can be done
about it, it's almost acceptable. There's no answer, and it's
frustrating. It's very frustrating for me, so I know it must be
frustrating for others, and I'm on a better level than most. But I
think my acceptance comes from myself – I accept I'll never get
beyond a good tolerance level. I'm very aware that I'm going to
fly off the handle about it. It's horrible thing to admit, but I'm
jealous of the escape. I'm not jealous of the clothes, I'm jealous of
what they get out of it.

Susan

Susan is 34. She has been married for fourteen years to Jeff, who
runs a small business. They have two sons, aged 8 and 4. They live in
a spacious, modern house in a village outside London. Susan
worked as an accounts clerk until the birth of their first child, and
now she handles the accounts for her husband's business. She came
across Jeff's transvestism by accident two years ago. He has been
cross-dressing since he was a teenager, using clothes belonging to
his sister and his mother, then buying his own. Susan told of her
discovery:

I couldn't make it out. I found cotton wool with bits of make-up in the bin upstairs in the bedroom. And if I ever came back unexpectedly, he was always in the bathroom and it took him a long time to come out. I was just pottering around in the boiler room one evening when he was out and I noticed this bag hanging down from the false ceiling. I pulled at it, and inside I found all these things – false boob things and panties and a pair of shoes. I was really distressed, I really didn't know what to do. I wasn't sure what to do: I wasn't sure whether to face him or just forget about it. When we went upstairs to bed I just confronted him. There was horror on his face, horror. He'd said to himself that if I ever found out that would be it, our marriage would be over.

Following this initial confrontation things started to fall into place for Susan. The realisation that Jeff had been cross-dressing throughout their marriage threw a different light on various events which, at the time, had puzzled her:

I remember once we went to a fancy-dress party where the men were supposed to dress as women. I never have liked that kind of thing, but he went dressed up and I wouldn't speak to him the whole of the evening. And of course he was chuffed as ninepence when he won first prize. That was when we'd been married four years, but it never twigged, you see. I didn't know this kind of thing went on.

I could never buy clothes on my own. He always wanted to be with me and he always wanted me to try on things that I would class as quite hideous, which I wouldn't do, and he'd get quite stroppy with me. Before we got married, he went absolutely berserk when I bought a pair of trousers. He only lets me wear trousers now because I know. I bought myself a pair the other day and he said, 'I don't like them.' But when I wore them on Saturday, he said sarcastically, 'Oh well, if you're wearing trousers, is it alright if I go in a dress?'

Matters came to a head on the way to a New Year's Eve party. While Susan was driving Jeff suddenly pulled on the brake and the car went off the road. He told her that he couldn't stand it any longer and she would have to see him dressed:

So the following day we were on our own because the children were staying with somebody, and he got dressed up in this mini-skirt thing, and insisted I should see him. I thought, 'My God, that's my husband! He doesn't look like my husband any more, he looks like a woman.' You see, the thing with Jeff is, if he's going to do something, he does it to the best of his ability. And when he dresses up, he really does. He's ever so figure-conscious, sometimes he won't eat very much at all. He's quite a slim build, and he shaves all his arms and all his legs.

Susan's discovery of Jeff's transvestism has made the situation worse. The fact that she now knows about it has encouraged him to cross-dress more often and spend more on clothes and going out. Communcation between them has deteriorated:

He's got a terrible temper and many a time I've thought, 'If he does anything else I'm going', because we've had smashed windows, things broken around the house. He has hit me – he's been violent to me, and I didn't know why – but I presume it was because of his dressing-up. He did say it was related to a certain extent; you know, when he couldn't get dressed. Now he has the option of dressing most of the time, but we're still getting the temper. I thought I could help him get over it, but it's only after months that I've realised what it involves and how much of his time it takes up. And I do feel sometimes it's as if he's holding a hammer over my head – 'Either you let me, or I'm going to get all moody and fed-up.'

Since I've known about it, the amount of money he's spent on clothes is unbelievable, and on make-up and wigs; and he's just bought some false boobs that cost him £150. The other day I found he'd bought a new skirt. He'd obviously gone into Selfridges and spent £20 on a new skirt. All this money and we're trying to save up for a holiday in France.

There's times when I wish I'd never known. It's got a lot worse since I found out. I thought it would be something that he desired doing about once a year, or once every six months, and that was it – it would be over and done with. I hadn't realised that it would be a thing where he virtually expects to go to London every Saturday. I think to myself, my husband's up in London every Saturday night, dressed as a woman, having a whale of a time, getting back at 5 o'clock in the morning, and here I am stuck indoors. The only way I can come to terms with it sometimes is to think that he's got another woman – you know, when he's going up to London, he's seeing somebody else.

Despite denials and reassurance from Jeff, Susan worries that either he is really gay, or that he may want to live full-time as a woman:

When we were first married, sex was OK. I suppose his sex drive is fairly low, but it was alright. I tell you the truth, he hasn't bothered with me virtually for two years. Ever since I found out, he just hasn't bothered. I mean, I did try him a couple of weeks ago, and nothing happened at all. I don't want to go to marriage guidance – there's no way I want to get involved with anyone like that.

He's convinced he's not gay, but the only time I've ever been up to London with him, he was being chatted up by a man there, and he looked like he was quite enjoying it. Now that quite worried me, but he tells me no way is he involved with any of them like that. I've said to him, 'In the years to come are you going to decide that you want to go the whole way?' And he says to me, 'Oh no, never.' But I know that he has thought about it, and I wonder if anything did happen to us whether that's what he would do.

When he's dressed up he's so different. He'll say to me, 'Would you like a cup of tea?', which he'd never think of doing normally. I mean he's a real chauvinist pig when he's not dressed, no kidding! Everybody used to comment on how he never used to help at all. Whereas other men would wheel a hoover round or help with the washing-up, he'd go and buy me a dishwasher to save him the hassle of trying to help me. I suppose, in a lot of respects, he's more of a reasonable person to talk to when he's dressed.

He knows I don't like it. I mean, he gets a lot of pressure from work, but there again, so do I. I get a lot of pressure as well – he never has a lot to do with the children – but there's no way I can just unwind. I mean, seeing him dressed up winds me up even more. It's very easy for him to come home and sit down and watch the television, and he says, 'Oh I think I'll just pop down the pub for a drink.' It's easy, he can go out dressed as a man. It's very difficult for me to get out; most of my friends are married with children and I can't just go out on my own.

The children are unaware of Jeff's transvestism and Susan is concerned about possible effects it may have on them, but she is also conscious of the difficulties faced by women on their own with children and she wants to keep the marriage together:

> I feel that he should have told me before we had children. I wish there was some research into it. I think it's got to be something genetic. I really do hope that it isn't. The children would have to be a lot older before they could be told. The eldest one would take it very seriously. I think he would be quite hurt. Jeff's got a couple of wigs on heads on top of the wardrobe, and I've said to him that he's going to have to do something with them because I'm afraid the children will notice them and wonder what they are. Also the fact that he keeps nail varnish on his toes all the time. I don't like it. I don't like him going around with nail varnish left on.
>
>   I have thought about leaving, but my sister has a broken marriage, and she's bringing up three children on her own, and I've seen what it's done to those children. I suppose in some respects I feel I couldn't do it to mine. I feel that if I can just grin and bear it – for the children's sake. You know, in a lot of respects – and I've said this to him – I do feel sorry for him, but he says, 'You don't want to feel sorry for me 'cos I've got the best of both worlds. I can see from a woman's point of view and I can see from a man's point of view.'
>
>   It goes in waves, really. Sometimes I feel I can cope quite well and other times I feel I'm just wasting my life. Once you've seen your husband dressed as a woman it's very difficult to forget. I think I still love him, but he's not the person I married. I still find it very difficult to accept. In actual fact, it's funny, but you feel you're not living with a man any more sometimes. It's just like having another woman in your house that you haven't invited in. It's just that it comes back to the fact that I married a man and I'm cheated. I've been cheated, you know.

Leonie

Leonie is 34 and has been married to Terry for thirteen years and

they have one daughter. Before her marriage Leonie was a
secretary, though she has worked as a part-time waitress in the past
few years. Terry is a lorry driver. A year ago she had major surgery
and has since been convalescing. Shortly after the wedding Terry
tried to let her know about his transvestism, but she didn't
understand. He suggested an evening of dressing up in her clothes;
Leonie agreed, and thought nothing more about it. A few years
later, Leonie came home early from work and found Terry in her
clothes and wearing make-up. He convinced her that he had simply
been trying it out for fun. And:

Then I fell pregnant with my daughter. I was pretty ill when I was
having her and I suppose I didn't take much notice of what was
happening around me, but things were disappearing – stockings,
underwear and a couple of dresses. And I used to think, 'What
the hell's going on?' I knew I hadn't mislaid them, yet I began to
doubt myself, because there was no explanation of where they
might've gone. Then Lyndsey was born and, of course, I suppose
I was a bit wrapped up in her. He kept disappearing upstairs, but I
really didn't take much notice of it.

My mother got really ill. I had to go and stay with her for a
month. I came back two days earlier than he expected me to, and
I think this is what really brought it to a head. When I got home he
was at work. I was just putting my things away when I saw a box in
the bottom of our wardrobe and, knowing it wasn't there before I
went, I opened it. Out came an inflatable doll, a full-sized doll, all
dressed up in my underwear. I screamed so hard, my neighbours
shot in the house. I managed to come out on the landing – I don't
know how – and I said, 'Its OK, I'm alright, I'm alright.'

When Terry came in I just blew up. I think it is the worst thing
for a woman to come up against, because you're no longer a
woman, you're no longer a wife, you're no longer a person,
you're compared with a lump of rubber. I just felt that he
preferred that to me. I can remember it distinctly, just staring at it
and thinking, 'God, is that what I am?' It was hideous, absolutely
hideous.

Leonie knew nothing about transvestism and could not understand
Terry's behaviour. Her stress increased because of the lack of
sympathy from other people:

I couldn't sleep, I couldn't eat, I couldn't do anything. I was like a walking zombie. I went to the doctor and he said, 'Tell your husband to come and we'll talk it out. Maybe there's some way we can help him, we can treat him to stop it.' So there's my doctor saying to me that it can be treated, it's a disease and there's something wrong with him, and Terry saying, 'There's nothing wrong with *me*, it's *you*.'

I remember my friend Sue saying, 'Oh, it's not that bad.' I said, 'OK, it's not that bad. I hope it never happens to you.' 'Oh,' she said, 'I wouldn't tolerate it.' But she still stood by Terry because she likes him. He's such a charming person and this is the hardest thing I had to fight – people wouldn't believe that Terry could be like that.

It wasn't just on the sexual side. That he put me through hell is an understatement – he tore me to shreds. He made me feel as if I was nothing. Believe me, that's not nice. He said that I was frigid, that I was no good as a woman. I couldn't do anything right; I couldn't cook, I couldn't iron. I had no confidence in myself, I used to cry night and day. My doctor said there was nothing wrong with me, that I was letting him sow doubts in my mind – which he had, because he was relentless. Believe me, I was nothing. I was a load of dirt. I had nothing in me, there was nothing. He had taken everything away.

Leonie's anxiety reached the stage where she was hospitalised, but this could not solve the problem of Terry's transvestism:

I remember going back and forth to the doctor, then I went into hospital – a bloody mental home. They said I had mental anxiety. They did all that ECG in your brain – evil thing. Then I paid out £280 to go and see a hypnotherapist to try to understand and accept this. But even the hypnotherapist turned round and said, 'Your mind has got a mental block, you'll never accept it.' I saw so many doctors – I saw a psychiatrist – and they all said to me, 'Get out. He's going to destroy you.' And even though I had all the proof there was nothing wrong with me, he still got to me every time. He still made me feel inferior and he cracked me up so many times.

He formed a friendship with Jane and Colin down the road. They know all about it and, again, I got blamed for it. I think there's something going on between her and Terry, even now. He moved in down the road, but he just would not leave me alone. He kept coming down here and having a go at me. He'd try to talk, try to sort things out. I'd be thinking to myself, 'Maybe I was wrong. Let's try again.' Then he'd come back with, 'You're frigid', or 'You never do this, you never think.' And instantly I'd be back to square one, a trembling heap and wreck again. I went and saw my solicitor and then Terry threatened he'd take Lyndsey off me. He threw it at me that I'd been in a mental home and said that no court will ever give you custody of a child if you've been in a mental home.

Like other wives, Leonie found that most support came from talking to someone in a similar situation:

Last year I got to the point I had taken enough. I couldn't take any more. It just clicked in me that he wasn't going to abuse me. From then on, I fought him and he never got an inch. He didn't even get half an inch. By this time, I'd had seven years of it. I knew that if I gave in that time I was finished: I'd be in a loony bin.

He started being nice again then, and said, 'Why don't you write to the Beaumont Society again?' I said no, because I wrote to them once before – and the ludicrous letter I got back from those stupid idiots! Obviously it was a transvestite, saying 'Why don't you encourage him, help him to dress?' Jesus, that was the last thing I needed! Anyway, I said 'OK, one more time.' At least I'd be able to say that I'd tried. So I wrote off and obviously they transferred it to Polly. I sat there reading this letter and I thought, 'How can she accept something like that when it's torn me to shreds all these years? How can this woman just write to me and say she understands how I feel?'

So really I was quite ready for a battle with Polly. We talked on the phone quite a lot, and I'll tell you, if I hadn't met Polly, there's no way my marriage would be together now, no way. If it hadn't been for Polly and knowing that there are other women in the same position, I wouldn't have made it. She's not very accepting of transvestism. She has to give the impression she is, because she's WOBS, so she can't turn round and say, 'I don't accept it. I think it's disgusting.' But deep down in her she's feeling as much anguish as we all are.

Now Leonie and Terry have reached an uneasy truce, but she is still in conflict about the situation. She is adamant that their daughter should not find out about the situation:

You can't say he's having an affair, but he is. He is having an affair with this fictional woman. That was one of the hardest things to try and sort out in myself – that he was doing this, that he was a woman at times. He asked me to have sex with him when he was dressed, but there's just no way I'd tolerate him like that. What he was doing, in a sense, was trying to introduce, not another woman into bed, but the make-up of another woman. No way could I accept that.

He does it once or maybe twice a week now, a couple of hours, maybe all evening. He dresses up in the bedroom and there's a lock, so there's no fear of Lyndsey walking in. I know what harm it's done me and I will never, ever let it anywhere near my daughter. She asked me why the wardrobe's locked and I just said there's Christmas presents in it. You see, Polly and Ron are very fortunate, they've got four children. But my daughter is on her own, she hasn't got a brother or a sister to discuss it with, she's only got me. I think being an only child, you can be harmed so easily.

Now I say how much he's going to spend on clothes. He doesn't have an unlimited budget because I don't allow it. If I didn't allow him to buy some of his own clothes, he'd only use mine, but no way would I ever let him touch my clothes again. I just don't want him touching my clothes.

At the present time I can't really say what I'm feeling, because of the operation. Matters were taken out of my hands. Since the operation I've seen another side of Terry. I don't say it's all nice – because it's not – but I have seen a change. But what I want to know is: when I'm better, is that change permanent, or is it just a temporary thing because I'm not well and he thinks he can manipulate me? I'll make a decision after I'm better. Maybe I will stay, I don't know. Even with all that's happened, deep down inside me I still love Terry. I think that's one of the hardest things. Even when I was going through hating him, the other part of me was loving him.

I used to think there was something wrong with me. I suppose it was his defence, his weapon, to say those things about me. In

many ways, I feel that this illness was meant to be, for the simple
reason that I have had time to myself, to understand myself and to
like myself again. When it's been drummed into you for nearly
ten years that you're not a nice person, that you're frigid and
you're not a good wife, you begin to believe it.
    I still don't understand the need for a man to dress up. I
understand Terry a bit better, I understand the need to go to
meetings, to feel they're not the only ones, that there are other
men who enjoy what they enjoy doing. But you can't accept that
he just wants to do this – there must be a reason behind it. I still
wish that it'll just disappear out of my life. I know it's not going to,
but there's always that little bit of hope that he'll wake up one day
and it'll never be part of his life again. But that's a false dream
really. It's the sort of dream I think all wives hang on to, if they're
truthful about it.

7

Transvestism and marriage

'I don't actually know why I feel like I do.'

(Polly, married to a transvestite)

It is perhaps significant that, while attending a large transvestite gathering in the USA, Beigel (1969) found that the number of divorced men was nearly double the national average, and almost all admitted that the reason for divorce was their wives' opposition to their cross-dressing. Their wives objected to their secret masturbation and their sexual demands as well as to the strain imposed on the family budget by the maintenance of an extra wardrobe. This latter aspect is highlighted by Beigel's report of the angry and horrified reaction of a woman who had accompanied her husband to the gathering and was highly distressed at seeing his new, expensive clothing bought with her earnings but without her knowledge. The husband's response was simply that transvestism worked for him as a form of therapy and relaxation, so she would have to put up with it.

As Prince and Bentler (1972) demonstrate from their survey of 500 transvestites, some women establish a level of acceptance and tolerance of their husbands' transvestism. Just under a quarter stated that their wives were understanding and co-operative, but, of course, mailed questionnaires are notoriously inaccurate. One can only speculate on the degree of wishful thinking which may have entered into the men's responses. Talamini (1982) reports that 60 per cent of his sample of wives accepted their husbands' cross-dressing. However, as his 'acceptance' category included wives who insisted that their husbands dress in private, it would be reasonable to treat this percentage rather sceptically. In the few pages devoted to women, it is unclear if they were interviewed alone, or together with their husbands, many of whom had already been interviewed by Talamini. Research and the interviews reproduced in the previous chapter suggest that an interview with a woman in the presence of her transvestite husband will elicit a considerably less candid response than if she is able to talk privately. Benjamin (1966) reports that very few wives enjoy helping a husband cross-dress or even seeing him in feminine attire. Nevertheless, they often do not want to see him looking a fright, deluding himself that he has become a beautiful woman, so some do help with clothes and make-up. Conversely, some men can and do transform themselves into attractive and convincing 'women', and this can give rise to feelings of insecurity in a wife who feels outdone and threatened – there is no longer anything special about her.

Benjamin is adamant that a woman should always be told prior to marriage about her husband's transvestism: unfortunately this does not happen in the majority of cases. He quotes Buckner's unpublished thesis which reports that 72 per cent of transvestites did not tell their wives before the wedding; similarly Talamini found that 60 per cent of the wives had not been told. Prince and Bentler found in their aforementioned survey that a fifth of wives were still unaware of their husbands' transvestism. Thus many wives find out after the marriage has taken place, the public statements have been made and possibly a family has been started. Some find out shortly after marriage, others not until many years have passed.

Where did I go wrong? – a question often asked by women when a marriage runs into difficulties, frightened that her husband may leave and thus destroy the tremendous emotional investment that she has made as wife, lover and homemaker. When the relationship is suddenly turned upside down by the discovery that the man she thought she knew is indulging in an activity which she does not understand, that she dislikes and knows little about, the shock can be intense. Compounded by the fact that she has no one to turn to, she is confused and alone.

Until recently there were no specialist groups in Britain to help the wife of a transvestite. She could only call on the Marriage Guidance Council, the Samaritans (a crisis helpline), or her doctor, which is one reason why attempts at giving advice to wives have

122   *Fantastic Women*

been initiated by transvestites themselves. In terms of published
reading material there is very little: *The Transvestite and His Wife*,
by Virginia 'Charles' Prince (1967), the transvestite organiser of the
Foundation for Full Personality Expression; and *Transvestism
Within a Partnership of Marriage and Families*, by Yvonne Sinclair
(1984), also a transvestite and organiser of the Transvestite/
Transsexual Support Group. Additionally there is a short pamphlet
published by WOBS (Women of the Beaumont Society) (n.d.), an
offshoot of the Beaumont Society which caters to heterosexual
transvestites.

Prince assures the wife that she is not to blame for her husband's
cross-dressing, but warns that she could indeed experience trouble
if she does not attempt to understand and accept. Here we have a
publication which tells us little about the wives themselves, but
much about how these wives should behave. Prince admits that the
book is one-sided, but given his claim that transvestite is the most
perfect example of humankind, this isn't surprising. The rationale
offered for such bias is that the reader will already have many
antagonistic views. Thus the book is an attempt to rectify the
balance.

Prince claims to have encountered few happier marriages than
those in which the wife fully accepts and participates in her
husband's transvestism, and, conversely, few more unsatisfactory
ones than those in which the wife rejects his behaviour and refuses
to accept. After all, the transvestite husband offers definite
advantages because he is more understanding of feminine needs and
desires: 'If a wife really comes to understand the feminine
personality within her husband she will have a fuller relationship
with her spouse than could otherwise be the case because she can
enjoy and live with both at the same time' (p. 48). The wife has both
a husband and a girlfriend in one person, because her husband goes
over to the wife's side and looks at the world from her point of view.

But what if the wife should fail to understand, or even inform her
husband that she cannot stand his behaviour? This, says Prince, is
an indication of her immaturity which stems from her own,
unresolved, emotional problems. As if to drive the point home,
Prince has reprinted an article from *Transvestia*, a magazine produced by The Foundation for Full Personality Expression. Entitled
'Wives A–F', it takes the six grades used to categorise American
school students' work and applies them to the wives of transvestites.

The 'A' (excellent) wife goes all out to understand and accept; she enjoys her husband's transvestism and actively encourages him, going out of her way to meet socially with other transvestites and their wives, so that it becomes as much a part of her life as it is his. 'She takes him without reservations because she loves him' (p. 69). The 'B' (good) wife takes a pragmatic attitude and, while not bothering to delve into explanations of the causes of transvestism, happily accepts her husband's cross-dressing, allows him to sleep in a frilly nightie, will shop with him for his clothes and accompany him when he is cross-dressed, 'but will not conceive of giving up a weekend with the children or at her sister's country house in preference to a TV weekend' (p. 70). The 'C' (average) wife is shocked when she first discovers that her husband is a transvestite but now she puts up with it, although she will not offer any encouragement; she puts on a brave front but is terrified of friends and neighbours finding out. She is the most common type. The 'D' (fair) wife will occasionally tolerate his cross-dressing but will try to reform him. She refuses to tell the children about their father and resents the money spent on clothes. In this case 'things are rougher for the TV', and 'If he should give her a kiss while he's dolled up, she'll freeze' (p. 73). For the 'D' wife there is only a 50/50 chance that the marriage will survive. The 'F' (failure) wife 'is a living hell for the TV', refusing to accept, and monitoring his behaviour and purchases in an attempt to stop him. She threatens to divorce him and to use his behaviour as grounds in court. 'I recently learned of a case in which the wife just walked out on her husband taking the children with her. She would not expose her little "angels" even for a minute to his perverting influence. The poor TV was actually in tears when he told me the story' (p. 76).

The wife's refusal to accept him as he is causes pain to the husband. For the wife to argue that he is causing *her* pain is wrong because, Prince feels, 'You are causing your own pain by taking an antagonistic rather than a sharing attitude . . . your discomfort is *self-inflicted*' (p. 42, emphasis added). The message is unmistakably clear: if you really love your husband you will not only accept his transvestism fully, you will also enjoy it. To complain of the hurt, rejection, humiliation or revulsion is silly and pointless because such feelings are self-induced. Prince offers advice: through enlisting her husband's help, a wife can easily graduate to become a class 'B' or even a class 'A' wife. And a salutory warning to those women who complain: Who wants to be a grade 'F' failure when they could try harder and become a grade 'A' high-flyer? One could dismiss *The Transvestite and His Wife* as fantasy, the wishful projections of some transvestites who want it all their own way. But imagine someone reading the booklet who has recently discovered her husband's transvestism, who is bewildered and isolated in her anxieties. What effect would it have on her? The difficulty is that the booklet has very little to do with real wives. Granted it contains letters (which may or may not be real) from wives who have come to terms with transvestism, but in the final analysis Prince dictates the required response: accept and enjoy – if you have any problems you only have yourself to blame.

In contrast, Sinclair aims to provide 'sound information and advice', admitting to being pro-transvestite, but also recognising that the transvestite can harm 'those whom they least wish to hurt' (p. 21). Linked with this approach, TV/TS has recently initiated a telephone helpline run by women for women, and a partners' group has been set up since moving into new premises. The first part of the booklet *Transvestism Within a Partnership of Marriage and Families* contains responses to questions typically raised by wives. Though considerably more detailed, in this respect it is similar to the pamphlet produced by WOBS which also follows a question and answer format. However, the theme is still basically that the transvestite cannot give up his obsession and that the wife must attempt to come to terms with it. Otherwise 'you will drive a wedge between yourselves until it leads to a future apart' (p. 10). In it, three wives briefly recount their experiences and, although they claim their husband's transvestism is not an insurmountable problem, it is clear, particularly in one case, that the present level of understanding has been reached through anguish and doubt. Unlike Prince, Sinclair retains a realistic grasp of the situation and refuses to side completely with the transvestite, even going so far as to instruct him not to abuse his wife's acceptance:

> Putting on a frock is not being a woman. Most of the time, for the average woman, the routine is pretty boring, and housework is a drudge. It might be fun for you to tie a scarf around your wig and then start dusting the shelves and mop the floor; she will have to follow you around afterwards and do it properly. (p. 35).

We come to the question: why is such gender-inappropriate behaviour so unacceptable in marriage? Why is a wife typically horrified at the sight of her husband dressed in female clothing, wig and make-up? Why does she dislike him shaving his arms and legs? Indeed, why is there a need for information and counselling services for women married to transvestites? Is the reaction generated by an absolute, rigid conception of gender which categorises feminine and masculine as total opposites? If this were the case, then presumably a non-sexist society would be able to incorporate transvestism with ease. Even as a hypothetical projection this seems unlikely, because transvestism does not mean becoming a woman in any sense of the term. Rather it entails putting on the trappings of femininity (often in a stereotypical manner with frilly or 'erotic' underwear, stilettos and heavy make-up), and relies on constructed appearance and masquerade. As such it bears little relation to reality as experienced by most women in everyday life. There is, it would seem, little payoff for the wife: her views of her marriage, her husband, her life receive a severe jolt when she discovers her husband's predilections. And even though a couple may reach a greater level of understanding in the long run, this can only occur if the wife is prepared to adjust to the situation. In many cases it is the wife who has to learn tolerance and acceptance if she wants to maintain her marriage. Person and Ovesey (1978) note that the success of a marriage is determined by the wife's capacity to tolerate cross-dressing as well as a low level of sexuality, and that the divorce rate is, in fact, high. Many transvestites are woefully unaware of the effects of their behaviour on their wives. Given the economic and emotional dependency of most women, adjustment may appear to be the only solution.

In contrast to this, Monica Jay (1985) found transvestism easy to accept, but significantly this occurred in a context of her own economic independence. She has recorded her affair with a younger transvestite in an autobiographical volume which she describes as a love story. Gerald/'Geraldine' came into her life initially as a guest in her boarding-house, separated from his wife who was unable to tolerate his cross-dressing. Soon they became lovers, with Monica a willing participant in his transvestite fantasies. She describes the affair as a great love, but in fact the whole book is about Gerald's needs and how she adapted to them and tried to fulfil them, sublimating her own needs:

I knew only too well how much he hated emotional scenes – throughout our affair I always had to be the stronger one, never allowing him to sense my sadness or despair. (p. 109).

When Gerald wanted humiliation and punishment, Monica had to force herself to do it. Nevertheless, she derived pleasure from his transvestism, as shown in the descriptions of their love-making with Gerald dressed in sexy, feminine underwear. She writes that when a transvestite friend, Alan/'Ann', and his wife Margaret came to dinner, Monica made Alan up to look glamorous. Margaret appeared threatened by this and so Monica made her up too. She then asked Margaret if she allowed 'Ann' to make love to her. Margaret was very upset by this as Alan's transvestism had recently come to light, after nearly twenty years of marriage. Monica's only comment on this is 'It had been a most eventful dinner party' (p. 82).

The prime focus is on Gerald/'Geraldine'. Monica invests such a depth of emotion in her relationship with him that when he leaves to follow a successful career abroad her heartbreak is devastating. She describes her love for him as being almost like the love of a mother for a child:

> He was my darling man, my lover, he was also the child I needed to protect from suffering and surround with love, helping him to become strong and resilient. (p. 780).

It is a sad book, a testament from a woman who gave all to a man's pleasure and well-being and is then left with pain and desolation. However, this scenario is not peculiar to affairs with transvestite men. The significant feature here is Monica's joyful acceptance of Gerald's transvestism. Suffice to say that this appears to be a rare phenomenon; certainly such reactions are not found among the majority of wives attending the Partners' Support Group at TV/TS. It could be argued that fully accepting wives (the grade 'A' wives according to Prince) are hard to find, simply because they do not need to attend a support group. However, none of the transvestites ever indicated the existence of such a wife at home. If they had, they would have been strongly encouraged by others to bring her to TV/TS meetings.

In terms both of their views of themselves and of their husbands' behaviour, most wives seem to be unhappy with the idea of their men masquerading as women. One of the difficulties here is that it is not always easy to differentiate between general problems in a marriage and those raised specifically by transvestism. Polly, for instance, commented that she and Ron had started living together more or less at the same time as she found out about his transvestism. She felt that difficulties would have arisen as the relationship settled down into a more mundane pattern regardless of the particular question of his cross-dressing. Eleanor found that her marriage was growing stale and that there was a distance between her and Will after years of raising a family. In some respects it seems that it was her discovery of Will's transvestism which ultimately brought them closer together, despite a long period of anguish. Similarly the onset of June's depression and feelings of anxiety did not coincide with George's admission of his love of feminine clothing but had started some while before. In fact her experience of breakdown and subsequent recovery could be seen as something which would have happened anyway. Susan also commented that her husband's outbreaks of temper had not improved once she knew about his transvestism; if anything, they had become worse. Leonie is possibly the only one of the five women whose problems can be seen as relating directly to the discovery of her husband's transvestism, but, even here, her illness intensified the situation. This is not to suggest that the difficulties experienced by these women were simply incidental: rather that some kind of crisis, in this case the discovery of a husband's cross-dressing, can bring other strains and problems to the surface.

A common theme uniting all the wives is their attachment to traditional notions of gender roles and appearance. Susan's comment that she married a man but now feels cheated, summarises the feelings expressed by all the women. They want their men to be men, and while ideas about gender roles are not specified they, nevertheless, have definite ideas about how a man should look and behave. By dressing as a woman the husband has failed to live up to expectations. While the wife may feel that her man has become less masculine she also feels, paradoxically, that his ideas of femininity and acting as a woman are out of touch with reality, bearing little relationship to her own experience. Susan recognised this when she referred to Jeff enjoying the best of both worlds: he enjoyed going to clubs as a woman, but was also able to slip down to the local pub for a drink as a man. In contrast Susan felt that she was trapped in the home, able only to go out when accompanied by her husband or a friend. Polly was critical of what she saw as posing – adopting a façade of femininity which bore little relationship to her daily life as a wife and mother – and also jealous of the apparent ease with which her husband could relax, simply by putting on a dress. So it could be argued that although the wives display fairly traditional expectations of masculinity and femininity, their complaint is not simply along the lines of wanting their men to be men. It goes further than this because they also recognise that the adoption of femininity by their men has very little to do with their own experience. Polly commented that 'it's like turning yourself into what you want', and Leonie referred to the fantasy woman. For them it is a kind of candy-floss-and-tinsel femininity which takes little or no account of the reality of women's lives as workers, wives and mothers.

A further variation on this theme can be found in the personality changes manifested by the husbands. The ability to relax by putting on female clothing has already been noted, but, more than this, some of the wives pointed to quite marked alterations in their husbands' behaviour. As Polly said, this change can be worrying. Susan found that her husband stopped acting like 'a chauvinist pig' and was willing to perform some domestic tasks which he would never do in his masculine role. June's husband, George, probably demonstrated the most dramatic about-turn in behaviour. Not only did he become helpful around the house when he was dressed, but he also became relaxed and peaceful and 'lovely to live with'. In this sense a wife may feel that she is living with two people and feel confused about her relationship with her husband. Susan remarked that it was like having another woman in the house, and thus it seems that when a man cross-dresses he actually becomes someone else in the eyes of his partner. This has been commented on in an article which stemmed from discussions in the Partners' Support Group at TV/TS:

Many women have commented that when their transvestite partner is dressed he is warmer, more open – more like a woman. It seems as if many transvestites can only express their gentler side when dressed. That makes me weep for the human race.

While gender roles – the macho men and the tender women – are perpetuated, then the tender [weaker???] sex will continue to be oppressed, and the macho sex will continue to be emotionally stunted. (*Glad Rag*, no. 34, p. 19)

Obviously this varies from couple to couple. The behavioural change may be slight or, as in the case of one wife who attends the Partners' Support Group, it may be extreme. This woman's husband becomes an entirely different person when dressed, not only in terms of dress and appearance but also voice, mannerisms, conversation and attitudes, to the extent that she has to refer to his male self in the third person along the lines of 'When John comes back could you tell him that the washing machine needs fixing'. Thus the situation arises for many wives where their husband is not the man they thought they married.

How, then, does this relate to the sexual politics of gender? Marriage itself has been castigated for actively maintaining the inequalities and restrictions of gender division. In the case of transvestism in marriage, it would be easy to say that it challenges those traditional constraints which serve only to repress and restrict, but, in the light of the wives' experiences, such comment would be facile. That some have suffered very real distress is undeniable and, even when they have reached some acceptable level of compromise, the pain and anguish they have gone through cannot be ignored. One apparently logical conclusion would be to say that transvestites should be prevented from marrying, but this takes us onto dangerous ground and opens up all sorts of undesirable possibilities. For example, if the transvestite is seen as psychologically disabled and, therefore, to be prevented from marrying, then it is only a small step to encompassing the physically disabled under the same rubric of prohibition. A more practical step and more compassionate view would be to stress the necessity of informing the woman about it prior to marriage. As Benjamin (1966) observes, 'No transvestite should ever marry a girl [*sic*] without telling her of his peculiarity beforehand' (p. 44). However, many may fear losing the woman they love in the face of such confession. Alternatively, as Polly pointed out, when two people are first together, such revelations often have little impact because they believe that love will overcome any difficulties. Transvestites often hope that marriage will put an end to their desire to cross-dress; additionally it can take quite some time for some wives to realise the extent of the problem and the depth of their husband's needs. Thus, although such confession may seem worthy, in fact its effect may be limited.

Perhaps more to the point is the lack of awareness on the part of transvestites. Many are either unaware of the effects of their behaviour on their wives or are unwilling to take responsibility for their actions. Transvestites and their partners alike often commented that the transvestite can be selfish, demanding fulfilment of his needs and desires. A greater level of consideration and awareness is called for on the part of the transvestites themselves. While partners' support groups can provide a necessary channel of communication and mutual self-help for the women involved, transvestites could perhaps give more consideration themselves to the effects of their behaviour on their marriage and family life.

In the case of TV/TS, the relationship between the Partners' Support Group and the managing committee exemplifies the conflict that can arise between different interest groups. The support group started at the end of 1986 on the initiative of a couple of women married to transvestites. The first few meetings explored the need for such a group and set some topics for discussion: finding out about a partner's transvestism, its effect on self-image, sexual problems. A telephone helpline was set up, enabling women to talk to women. Although the discussion meetings were well attended and many women found them beneficial, disagreement arose concerning the necessity of confidentiality. Most women felt that details should remain within the meeting, but it soon became apparent that this was not being observed by all members. The problem was inflated by transvestite members of TV/TS objecting to the confidentiality rule; and also failing to respect the privacy of the group by walking into meetings. As a result, some women felt constrained and unable to express their feelings. A meeting between the group and committee representatives reached some compromise but the outcome remains to be seen, especially as some women feel that meetings should be held in other premises. Although the majority of women who attended the group were concerned to develop a deeper understanding of transvestism, the transvestites themselves appeared to feel both threatened by the existence of a discussion group which expressly excluded them and unable to accept the possibility that sharing problems can be constructive. It sems that while the committee was expecting the partners' group to prioritise support for the transvestites, the women felt that mutual support within the group came first. This conflict of perspectives is expressed by a member of the support group:

> What is upsetting is the fact that many TV's apparently feel that they are conferring an honour on their wives/girlfriends by wishing to appear as women and this in some way means that they are even more privileged when they wish to be she more than they are he. (*Glad Rag*, no. 31, p. 9)

What emerges here is that, despite the apparent conflict between the transvestites' needs and the claims being made by their wives for sympathy and understanding, both groups want support. Usually the transvestite is not searching for a cure, and even if one were readily available many would choose not to take it. Nevertheless, their behaviour is socially proscribed and stigmatised, so although they derive pleasure from cross-dressing, they are not entirely happy with themselves either. Why else would so many transvestites attempt to stop what they do – by throwing away all their feminine garments, getting married, growing a beard, immersing themselves in work or hobbies – if they did not feel some discomfort with their behaviour? Furthermore, at TV/TS the men thought that the Partners' Support Group was there to support *them*, the transvestites – an interesting interpretation of the group's name and purpose. The women, in contrast, needed each other's support and most expressed relief at being able to talk about their feelings and exchange experiences with other women in similar situations.

Clearly any notion of breaking down gender divisions finds little resonance in the views of many women married to transvestites. The wives featured in the previous chapter held on to fairly traditional notions of gender roles and behaviour; some women at the Partners' Support Group were more feminist, but, feminist or not, the problem is generally seen in personal terms: my man, my marriage, my family. In a society where gender divisions run deep it is unrealistic to expect women to sacrifice what they see as their happiness for the sake of an anti-sexist future. What the women in the last chapter and in the group wanted was a happy marriage and, for many of them, that also entailed the playing-out of traditional gender roles. On this level, then, the solution lies with the provision of sympathetic support and counselling, both by disinterested parties – the knowledgeable professionals – and by people with direct experience of either being or living with a transvestite.

One of the complaints commonly voiced by wives recalling their discovery of their husbands' transvestism is that they did not know where to turn, who to ask or who to phone. Given the stigma attached to transvestism, wives often fear that this will rub off on them, along the lines of, 'Well, they'll think I'm stupid/weak/ pathetic/perverted to want to stay with him.' Thus it becomes difficult for women to find out about the little support that does exist, and this difficulty is intensified by their fear of ridicule and censure. Often when faced with problems they may turn to family, friends or their doctor for help and advice, but they are less likely to do so in the case of a husband's transvestism. Consequently women need a counselling service which operates in their interest.

Peo (undated) writes that wives of transvestites find most support from women in the same situation, but the difficulty lies in finding other women. Once a woman has discovered her husband's transvestism there may follow a period when she is unlikely to know of any such contacts or organisations, and if the news has come as a shock to her, she may feel even more isolated and alone. He points out that all transvestites have direct experience of the anxiety and isolation that goes with this behaviour, especially in the early years. How then does a woman feel, especially if she has been unaware of it during many years of marriage? The husband himself is too close to the situation to deal with his wife's fears, worries or possibly anger in a calm, objective manner. He may not know much about transvestism himself. He may even worsen the situation by claiming that he knows what it's like to be a woman.

In Britain, transvestites have TV/TS, and its helpline and magazine; the Beaumont Society; special events like drag balls; various specialist shops and mail-order services; and hotels providing transvestite weekends. In the United States there are many more organisations devoted to promoting transvestite interests and providing support. In contrast there is very little for the wife who wants impartial information and advice, the opportunity to talk to other women and not be judged for staying with her husband. There are important 'sticking points'; among those commonly mentioned are frequency of 'dressing', shaving arms and legs, wearing frilly underwear under masculine clothes, wearing nail varnish on toes, pierced ears, going out frequently, money. Hard-and-fast rules cannot be made: while one woman may tolerate the nail varnish, she may hate the shaved legs; another will be less bothered by this than by the neighbours seeing him when he goes out 'dressed'. This can only be worked out between partners; hence there is a great need for knowledgeable counselling and discussion/support groups for both partners, together and separately.

Conclusion

Transvestism and the politics of gender

Liberalism and control

The debate concerning the causes of transvestism continues, but one thing is clear – there are no readily available means of curing it. Even if the causal factors were to be identified, how would they be used? Attempts to prevent transvestism developing, whereby manifestations of childhood and juvenile 'incorrect' gender behaviour are subject to modification by experts, reveal the slippery slope from intervention to control. More to the point, the underlying assumption is made that transvestism is problematic in and of itself. It is categorised under the heading of sexual deviance, or worse, and therefore something which must be eliminated, or at least kept at a relatively low incidence.

Strictly speaking, transvestism is not a medical condition in terms of being an illness requiring diagnosis, treatment and cure. However, along with other forms of sexual deviance it has been medicalised, treated as if abnormal and needing medical care. While transsexuals welcome medical interest as a means to achieving their goal of surgical sex change, the transvestite accepts his biological sex and does not generally require any sort of medical intervention. The medicalisation of a particular way of behaving simultaneously legitimates the idea of it as unacceptable and the attempt to eradicate it.

Curiously, transvestism is often presented as something which lies outside of the transvestite's control. He is depicted as a victim of drives or a psychological disorder with no choice but to act as he

134

does. Thus, on the one hand, it is suggested that transvestism is something which can be successfully prevented in childhood; on the other, gender identity and role constancy are presented as fixed – that masculinity is something which can be almost imposed on the individual. In no way is the transvestite seen as someone who makes choices and decisions.

These contradictory notions of masculine gender identity and role as both fixed and flexible are also found in transvestite self-imagery. From the transvestite point of view, cross-dressing should not be socially unacceptable: the problem stems from negative and uninformed attitudes, it does not lie with cross-dressing itself. Cross-dressing is seen as a solution, providing release and an outlet for suppressed frustrations, which surely is more acceptable than recourse to alcohol or violence? Here we see the attempt to normalise the transvestite which, in contrast to the medical model, argues that the transvestite has very little wrong with him – he is a normal masculine male, the only difference being that he likes to dress in female clothes from time to time. The problem lies with an intolerant society which cannot accept that his behaviour is something harmless and inoffensive.

At the same time, the transvestite is engaging in something which is socially condemned, stigmatised and ridiculed, and this causes him anxiety or worse, especially if he is isolated from other transvestites. Despite their claims for normalising cross-dressing, transvestites also depict themselves as suffering from an obsession or a form of compulsive behaviour over which they have little control. This, they say, is evidenced by the failure to effect a self-cure, despite the fact that most have attempted this at least once, often many times, by 'purging' – throwing away all their feminine gear – growing a beard, taking up time-consuming hobbies or work, getting married and so on. Conceivably this may have worked for some, but if it has they remain a hidden population. Seeing transvestism as uncontrollable allows the individual to rationalise his role, along the lines of 'I can't help it'. In Chapter 3 Lucy comments that transvestism is 'like drugs', seeing it as an addiction which cannot be conquered. Like the addict, the transvestite will be gripped by habitual behavioural patterns which, while causing distress, also provide considerable pleasure. Not surprisingly a lot of transvestites, like a lot of addicts, do not want to be cured.

The collective self-image, then, is contradictory. On the one hand, transvestism is no big deal, simply involving men who wish to extend the frontiers of masculinity and engage in gender bending. However, it runs foul of social ideas about what is right and proper. On these grounds he *should* be allowed to engage in cross-dressing. On the other hand it is something outside of the individual's control, a compulsion, an obsession which he cannot control and which cannot be cured. On these grounds he *must* be allowed to continue as he wishes.

The contradictions in both medical and transvestite models of gender underline the ways in which transvestism illustrates the social construction of gender. Masculinity is treated as a thing in itself, something to be achieved by all men. Those who do not evince a convincing image of masculinity have failed and, in the common parlance of insult, they become effeminate. It is no accident that transvestites are commonly thought to be homosexual; after all, any man who is effeminate cannot be heterosexual, there must be something 'wrong' with him. The treatment of children diagnosed as 'cross-gender identified' incorporates much of this thinking. It has been suggested that children who identify with the opposite gender should receive therapeutic treatment on two grounds (Zucker, 1985). First, this may forestall a later psychosexual outcome such as transvestism or transsexualism. Second, it may prevent rejection by the child's peer group in the more immediate situation. Both claims are vague and unsubstantiated but the important point here is that the children who are diagnosed as cross-gender-identified are usually boys.

In a discussion of their treatment of 'deviant sex-role behaviour' in a boy, Rekers and Lovaas (1974) identify masculine activities as aggressive, and state that any apparently feminine traits (such as playing with dolls, exhibiting feminine gestures) should be eradicated. In other words, masculinity is displayed through aggression which in turn demonstrates the absence of the feminine. Rather than reinforcing other masculine behaviour characteristics, the so-labelled feminine is eradicated and replaced by aggression. Nordyke *et al.* (1977) point out that the definition of deviant masculine behaviour is equated with what is considered to be traditional feminine behaviour. It is clear that the construction of gender is such that women may attempt to take on some of the trappings of masculine privilege and even play according to the boys' rules, with the proviso that they retain femininity and defer to men. However, woebetide the male who takes that downward step into femininity. Femininity is a poor second, it stands for everything that masculinity is not, and as a microcosm of the wider society and its dominant values, the family recreates this pattern.

Normal boys are aggressive, girls are not. Therefore, the boy who fails to display aggression and also plays with dolls has got something wrong with him, and thus something must be done about it because he may be rejected by his peers and he may grow up to be a transvestite or transsexual. This poses a sort of conundrum because, while the fixity and traditionalism of thinking here upholds all the bastions of patriarchy and male dominance, it is possible that the child may be suffering. Zucker is not clear about peer-group rejection, but most children experience it at some time or another in varying degrees. It is one thing to identify a socially ostracised child and to act accordingly; quite another to act on the basis of a guess that he might be shunned in the future. Clearly the thinking behind therapy for gender-identity problems is long overdue for analysis, and the possibilities of viewing the situation in alternative ways must be considered.

The other side of the coin here involves the transvestites themselves. Although they derive pleasure from their activities, they also suffer because of social pressures. Is it right, then, to deny the possibility that this problem could be prevented in the first place from ever arising; that through the provision of gender-identity clinics, there need be no more transvestites (or transsexuals)? Such an ethical question is irrelevant here, because prevention is not only impossible, it is also likely to remain so. We no more know why a person becomes transvestite than why they become heterosexual, lesbian or homosexual. Moreover, the scenario evoked by supposedly preventive techniques is a denial of the diversity of human social behaviour. On this level, then, the case must be made for tolerance and a change in social attitudes, through education and greater publicity for such a minority.

But the contradiction does not stop here. Transvestism is often private but it is not entirely isolated, because it can involve partners. We have seen that they do face difficulties and problems and that these must be recognised and not merely swept under the carpet in the quest for greater liberalism and tolerance. Again, this points away from stepping up the search for some cure in the interests of eradicating this form of behaviour. Transvestites are not beating down the doors of medical and psychiatric establishments, nor are they likely to. What they and their partners need is contact with supportive peer groups. Secrecy and isolation breed anxieties and it is organisations such as TV/TS which have attempted to fill a gap in organisations catering to sexual minorities. On a national level, facilities are still pretty thin on the ground and there are few centres for such groups. Self-help seems to be the major pathway for the provision of these facilities – the fund-raising campaign by TV/TS which led to the establishment of the new premises is one such example – but there also needs to be more widespread recognition of the problem, encompassing not only the transvestites themselves, but also the needs of their partners. Family doctors, therapists and counsellors are generally uninformed, both about transvestism and the relevant sources of advice and support.

Fantasy and feminism

Transvestism involves switching roles and identity, not only from masculine to feminine but also from reality to fantasy. Regardless of causes and reasons, transvestism is a fantasy, a means of projecting oneself into a different way of being, becoming another sort of person on a temporary basis. A fantasy world is limitless in its possibilities and the individual can fashion it as he wishes. The transvestite constructs an image, or images, of himself by dressing up, wearing make-up, creating a hairstyle, in just the same way that women do, but he uses it to become another person. He adopts another name, he may speak differently, he may even behave in a way which is 'out of character' with his more usual male self. Although it is more common for transsexuals to claim that they know what it is to be a real woman, some transvestites also argue this, which often irritates their partners. In this respect transvestism becomes something more than simple fantasy: it's almost as if some transvestites consider they are doing women a favour by pretending to be them. Elaine says that she likes women so much she wants to be one, a partner complains that they think they are 'conferring an honour' on their wives and girlfriends by appearing in feminine guise.

However, this claim to be partly feminine, to have experience of being a woman, rings false for two reasons. First, it seems that transvestites see gender as something which is rigidly demarcated – there is masculinity and there is femininity and they do not overlap. The behavioural changes in some men, as noted by their wives, bear testimony to this conceptual separation of roles. So although a lot of men engage in 'feminine' behaviour, in the case of the transvestite, he feels that this necessitates the wearing of feminine clothes and the construction of a feminine identity. It is almost as though this identity has to be put on before permission can be granted to do supposedly feminine things – from housework to being more emotionally open. In this respect, transvestism reflects traditional gender roles whereby masculinity and femininity are entities in and of themselves, mutually exclusive and fixed. The transvestite is maintaining gender divisions, making the statement through his behaviour, that a man can only engage in non-masculine behaviour if he first camouflages his masculinity and overlays it with the appearance of femininity.

The second reason returns us to this question of fantasy. What does a transvestite create when he cross-dresses? All appearance is a statement: we use it to say things about ourselves and our relationship to the world. As shown in Chapter 1, appearance is a non-verbal system of symbols which convey to others an array of meanings. However, the transvestite goes beyond this and, through the process of cross-dressing, creates someone else; someone who has a different gender and appearance, another name and sometimes another personality as well. In Chapter 4 we saw that Buckner (1970) portrays transvestism as a form of protection, shielding the individual from the reality of interpersonal, sexual relations. Through cross-dressing the transvestite creates a synthetic woman and, in doing so, he replaces actual reality with a synthetic reality. Transvestism comprises a 'synthetic dyad' in which his creation, his feminine self, responds to the wishes and desires of his masculine self. Thus he substitutes synthetic sexual relations for real human ones.

This analysis connects with the image of the TV as someone who derives sexual pleasure from cross-dressing, who masturbates while dressed and enjoys watching himself in a full-length mirror. It ties in with the fetishism referred to by Elaine, when she stole clothes from a washing-line, and it reflects Candy's satisfaction with the period when she lived alone and dressed every night, happy to be alone with her two selves. In this respect transvestism is redolent of some ways of using pornography, whereby the model looks directly at the camera and, therefore, at the purchaser. Regardless of what he does, the compliant, sexual image in the picture remains objectified and controllable. Similarly, for the transvestite, the feminine creation complies with his wishes, thereby enabling him to avoid the problems of a real relationship, the fear of rejection, the unpredictable, the lack of control.

It would seem that this analysis can only be partial, because it fails to account for the transvestite who wishes to have sex with his partner while dressed as a woman. In all cases wives reported that their husbands had suggested this to them, but most refused to go along with it. June did once, but disliked it; Eleanor felt that it was like going to bed with another woman. Monica Jay (1986) not only went along with Geraldine's wishes, but also enjoyed it, and joined him in dressing up in feminine sexy underwear. Undoubtedly there are other women who enjoy this too, but they are an invisible population. The point here is that the transvestite who wants to have sex with his partner while dressed does not simply find satisfaction in dressing and masturbating. He may still do this, but he also wishes to step out of this sexual fantasy world, and relate sexually to another person. Does this then invalidate Buckner's claim for the synthetic dyad replacing real relations? Probably not, because the transvestite is still relating to his partner through his fantasy. He would rather relate to her as his fantasy self than as his real self.

Stoller (1976) has suggested that, as a form of sexual behaviour, transvestism operates in much the same way as other forms of fetishism: that is to say, it depersonalises the partner. Extending this, Wise and Meyer (1980) argue that cross-dressing limits the full experience and enjoyment of interpersonal sex, and thus 'if one could help these individuals to experience others without the need for props, treatment is clearly justified' (p. 126). Is it puritanical to claim that the ability to enjoy 'propless sex' is necessarily better? Wise and Meyer have joined that large body of sexologists and experts who pronounce on sexual enjoyment, failing to recognise that it is impossible to legislate on the experience of pleasure.

In any case, the debate does not stop here because there are also transvestites who claim that cross-dressing is not a sexual experience for them. In the past, when they were younger, it was, but now the sensation is one of satisfaction and relaxation, a feeling of well-being, which does not automatically go hand-in-hand with any sexual activity. Polly's husband Ron, for example, would fall into this category. Certainly the wish to substitute for reality in a sexual context is not applicable here, but it appears that the transvestite is still only able to relax and feel at ease by becoming someone else. In this sense the substitution of reality remains.

A further aspect of gender arises: why do men, but not women, want to create this kind of fantasy figure? Why do some men experience such discomfort with their gender role that they are unable to incorporate change within it, that they have to shed that role completely and step into another? One way to examine this is to consider the question of socialisation and the sexual politics of gender.

Statham (1986) comments that while tomboy behaviour in pre-adolescent girls meets with social approval, boys' gender role behaviour does 'not have to stray far to cause concern for their psychological well-being' (p. 87). In a study of child-rearing practices, Statham found that it was considered easier to bring up girls than boys in an anti-sexist manner. Because males as a whole occupy a privileged position in society, bringing up a boy to be anti-sexist means that he must be taught to forgo certain advantages, and parents were unwilling to sacrifice their sons' futures to feminist ideals. In contrast, bringing up girls in this way calls for an opening-up of options and for constant encouragement, a process which parents found very much easier. Thus, although women and girls may be encouraged to make some headway into masculine domains, the reverse pathway is discouraged. Boys are brought up to embrace masculinity, and they meet with parental and social consternation when they exhibit signs of deviation from this developmental route – hence the imbalance of boys receiving treatment for gender 'inappropriate' behaviour.

This sheds some light on a paradox posed by transvestism. It is a one-way process, whereby men engage with feminine imagery, using it for sexual satisfaction, relaxation and pleasure. Patriarchal ways of thinking frown upon men being 'cissy', and, taken to the extreme of gender divisions, this means that any deviation from masculine behaviour traits and a manly appearance will be met with disapproval, censure and ridicule. Indeed the language of insult describes a rather fussy man as being 'an old woman', and assumes that all homosexual men are 'effeminate'. i.e. something less than real men, feminine. In contrast to this, when women break through the restrictions surrounding their ascribed status they often take on some aspects of behaviour traditionally associated with masculinity, like assertiveness or having a career. In doing so, they do not become anything other than women. It is often said that if a woman wants to succeed in a man's world she has to be better than a man. However, this does not require her to become a man – quite the reverse in fact; the image of power dressing is one which tempers efficiency with femininity. In other words, unlike masculinity, the construction of femininity does not call for a gender identity so inflexible as to reject the incorporation of behaviour traditionally associated with the opposite sex, precisely because masculinity is defined as superior. Moreover, the construction of sexuality does not associate masculine clothing with eroticism. For these reasons, then, transvestism is a phenomenon reserved for men.

Just why some men should take this division of masculinity and femininity to such extremes that they experience the need or even compulsion to become 'women' in order to express themselves, is debatable. The theories, as noted in Chapter 4, are numerous and varied. However, it is clear that without some notion of gender as a hierarchy, which demonstrates the primacy and prestige attached to masculinity, it is impossible to explain much about transvestism at all. In the first place, the concept of hierarchy permits a consideration of the social reactions to transvestism. A man dressed as a woman, outside of the close confines of entertainment, carnival or party, is met with derision. Such disregard for privileged status is as shocking as it is socially unacceptable. Similarly an understanding of gender clarifies the tendency for most transvestites to prefer an appearance of extreme femininity, complete with stilettos, frilly underwear and tight clothes. This kind of appearance complies with the male fantasy of female sexuality, the image of the whore, not the madonna. Finally it permits an understanding of the behavioural changes associated with cross-dressing by pointing to the fact that certain traits are out of bounds for 'real men', and although some are changing these stereotypes, others are unable, or unwilling, to incorporate these traits into their normal lives. For a minority, these traits are associated with, and expressed through, the construction of an alternative gender identity.

Public policies or private morals?

Talamini (1982) observes that transvestites in the USA are increasingly defining themselves as a sexual minority, subjected like other minorities to the injustices of prejudice and bigotry. He argues that their status is indeed that of a minority group discriminated against by 'a dominant class emphasizing excessive masculinism' (p. 58). Talamini's analysis here accords with the foregoing description of the transvestite as one who flouts the conventions of masculinity, thereby exposing himself to sanction and censure. But this does not go far enough. While the transvestite goes against the unwritten rules of masculinity, he does little to diminish their power. Indeed, it could be argued that at times the transvestite actively upholds patriarchal notions of women through his reliance on stereotyped images of femininity and sexuality. Monica Jay (1986) writes that her lover Gerald's enjoyment of humiliation and punishment included being 'forced' to cross-dress. Acting out his fantasy of being caught as an intruder in his landlady's bedroom, Monica then has to think of a suitable punishment:

> Trying hard to keep a cool head I searched for a way. Suddenly, in a flash, I had an idea – this should do it! If I was to turn this wretched man into a woman, surely this would be the best punishment of all? (p. 60)

What is significant here is not the sexual games that Monica and Gerald play and enjoy, but the fact that being forced to dress as a woman can be construed as a form of punishment. Given the social construction of gender, this does not work in reverse. Being forced to dress as a man – in underpants, socks, shirt and so on – could not be a punishment for a woman: it would be laughable, not humiliating. It is also highly unlikely that it would serve as a means of sexual stimulation, given that a dominant-female/passive-male scenario generally calls for sexually stereotyped accessories, like stockings and suspender-belts, thigh-high boots or stilettos.

More indirectly, this example also further emphasises the fact that transvestism is fantasy. Thus the question arising here is, can we expect fantasy behaviour to serve what are essentially political interests? One of the concerns of feminism is the construction of gender, which upholds the superiority and power of masculinity over femininity. Expectations that a feminist transvestism might emerge, or even that transvestism might chip away at patriarchal institutions and behaviour, are not only unrealistic but, like transvestism itself, they too belong in the realms of fantasy.

Transvestism does not mean becoming a woman. It does not even mean becoming a woman on a temporary basis. It relies on contrived appearance and a masquerade which bears little relation to most women's experiences of daily life. It says nothing about the sexual division of labour, still less about the dangers posed to women by male violence. The complaints voiced by wives of transvestites are not simply along the lines of wanting their men to be men. They felt that the kind of femininity portrayed by their husbands' cross-dressing was nothing to do with their own lives as women, wives and mothers. In fact, they felt that it was quite the opposite of their own lives, an escape from the everyday pressures. As Polly said, 'It's like turning yourself into what you want.' For some wives this is like living with two people; both Susan and Leonie expressed feelings of their husbands having affairs with another woman, all referred to behavioural and personality changes.

Talamini (1982) has suggested that transvestism demonstrates the fragility of the social fabric. We take its social construction for granted when, in fact, it can fracture all too easily. In one sense he is correct to assert that transvestism allows us to consider the social construction of gender in terms of roles, identities and appearances, but he fails to take this far enough. What we also find is that transvestism itself is a form of fractured behaviour which maintains masculinity and femininity as separate, exclusive entities.

The choice facing us here is not a simplistic one between liberal tolerance or moral repression, nor need we lapse into relativism and atomised individualism whereby each person ideally makes their own choices in accordance with their own tastes. An activity which is harmless and which satisfies the protagonists cannot be condemned out of hand; after all, if some men want to dress up as women, meet together and enjoy parties, drag balls and so on, what advantage is there in railing against it? From a feminist standpoint it may be argued that such behaviour is largely irrelevant to the purposes and concerns of feminism anyway. The claims made by some transvestites and others that cross-dressing is a contribution to the feminist cause are misplaced, but realistically it is unlikely to do it any harm either. Undoubtedly transvestism replicates gender divisions; it relies on images of women which have been used to objectify and oppress them. The transvestite uses this as fantasy for his own pleasure, always retaining the facility to return to the primary status of masculinity. In this sense it upholds the supremacy of masculinity, but when considered in comparison with the whole panoply of patriarchal representations in everyday life, it rather fades into insignificance.

It would be convenient if we could leave the debate there, but as with most things, transvestism is neither as simple nor as straightforward as that. In the first place, some transvestites experience anguish and anxiety as a result of social condemnation of their behaviour. Secondly, and importantly, there is a hidden population, the wives, many of whom are privately distressed by their husbands' behaviour. The case for transvestism relies on a greater moral diversity which in turn permits more freedom of expression. However, nothing can be achieved if the case for one group is advanced at the expense of another – in this instance by defending transvestism without equal consideration for the largely unvoiced and unheard interests of the wives. It is only within this framework of balance that the case for tolerance can be made.

Notes and references

Chapter 1: Seeing is believing? Sex, gender and appearance

1. The marriage of April Ashley, a post-operative transsexual, to Arthur Corbett, a biologically male transvestite, was annulled in the British courts. The judges ruled that the respondent, Ashley, was male, on the basis of previous gonadal and hormonal sex and unchanged chromosomal sex. See Fallowell and Ashley (1982).
2. R. Bogdan (1974) p. 96.
3. M. Brake (1976) p. 184.
4. This is clearly demonstrated in Elena Belotti's study of socialisation processes: *Little Girls* (Readers and Writers Publishing Collective, London, 1976).
5. The stricter confines of masculine socialisation have been outlined by Ruth E. Hartley: 'Sex Role Pressures and the Socialisation of the Male Child', in J. H. Pleck and J. Sawyer (eds), *Men and Masculinity* (Prentice-Hall, London, 1974); also by Andrew Tolson: *The Limits of Masculinity* (Tavistock, London, 1977).
6. It must be stressed that I am referring only to periodic cross-dressing here and not to the desire to become, physically as well as socially, a member of the opposite sex. Female-to-male transsexuals do exist, but they are greatly outnumbered by their male counterparts.
7. In Britain the most commonly used law in this respect is the Public Order Act (1936) Section 5. The law was originally enacted to deal with fascist street fighting in the 1930s, but has subsequently been used against cross-dressed men apprehended in public places, particularly women's toilets. The cross-dressed male using a men's public toilet may be arrested for homosexual importuning under the Sexual Offences Act (1956).

Chapter 2: Through the looking glass

1. See D. King (1981).
2. See J. Weeks (1981).
3. D. Fallowell and A. Ashley (1982) p. 75.
4. For a historical and cross-cultural overview of cross-dressing, see P. Ackroyd (1979).

5. C. S. Ford and F. A. Beach, *Patterns of Sexual Behaviour* (Harper, New York, 1951).
6. Prince (1957) would argue that the transvestite is typically heterosexual, a claim reflected by the Beaumont Society in Britain which is modelled on similar lines to the Foundation for Full Personality Expression set up by Prince in the USA. However, as both these organisations exclude homosexuals it is difficult to assess the accuracy of Prince's claim. During research I met heterosexual, homosexual and bisexual transvestites (according to their own definitions).

Chapter 3: Best of both worlds? Transvestite lives

1. This is dealt with in more detail in Chapter 4.

Chapter 4: The boy can't help it: scientific views of transvestism

1. By way of contrast it is worth noting the ways in which debates about male homosexuality were transformed through leaving the medico-psychiatric paradigm. See M. Spector and J. I. Kitsuse, *Constructing Social Problems* (Cummings Publishing, California, 1977) pp. 17–20.
2. Transsexualism was coined as a *diagnostic* label in 1966 by H. Benjamin (*The Transsexual Phenomenon*). Transvestism has been largely ignored in sociological research, the focus being predominantly on transsexualism. See H. T. Buckner (1970, 1971), D. Feinbloom (1976), D. King (1981).
3. Given the apparent lack of success reported in documented evidence one can only assume the existence of a large pool of unpublished, wholly unsuccessful research.
4. This process applies particularly to clinics established in the USA. See S. McNeill (1982) and J. Raymond (1980). The medicalisation of deviant behaviour, particularly sexual deviance, not only legitimates control but also, especially in the USA, provides the means to financial gain. See D. B. Billings and T. Urban (1982).
5. E. Person and L. Ovesey (1978) argue that transvestism is a case of 'gender disturbance' rather than sexual perversion. Despite their reservations and criticisms of the traditional Freudian formulation, they continue to view transvestism as stemming from pre-oedipal and oedipal conflicts.
The use of the term 'perversion' in this section refers simply to the psychoanalytical use of the term and does not entail any derogatory intention on the part of the author.
6. S. Jordan (1973); N. M. Fisk (1974).
7. As pointed out by D. King (1981) p. 179.
8. See V. Prince (1967).
9. S. McNeill (1982).

Chapter 5: Transvestism and women

1. A shortened version of this and the following chapter appears in *Women's Studies International Forum 1986*, 8, 6, pp. 583–92.
2. See Val Binney, *Leaving Violent Men* (Women's Aid Federation, London, 1981).
3. Olive Leonard, 1982 unpublished dissertation, South Bank Polytechnic, London.
4. D. H. Barlow and W. S. Agras (1973).
5. J. B. Bastani and D. K. Kentsmith (1980).
6. T. N. Wise, C. Dupkin and J. K. Meyer (1981).
7. See R. J. Stoller (1971); A. Storr (1964).

Chapter 6: Wives talking

1. D. Feinbloom (1976) was criticised by her research subjects for doing this. J. Talamini (1982) interviewed women in the presence of their husbands, which may explain the apparently high rate of acceptance. See Chapter 7.

Bibliography

Ackroyd, Peter, *Dressing Up. Transvestism and Drag: The History of an Obsession* (New York: Simon & Schuster, 1979).

Allen, Clifford, *A Textbook of Psychosexual Disorders*, 2nd edn (London: Oxford University Press, 1969).

Armstrong, C. N. 'Transvestism', in D. Robertson Smith and William M. Davidson (eds), *Symposium on Nuclear Sex* (London: Heinemann, 1958).

Ball, J. R. B., 'Transsexualism and Transvestitism' (2), *Australian and New Zealand Journal of Psychiatry*, 1, 4, (1967) pp. 188–95.

Ball, J. R. B., 'Transsexualism and Transvestitism (2), *Australian and New Zealand Journal of Psychiatry*, 2, 1, (1968) pp. 24–32.

Barahal, Hyman S., 'Female Transvestism and Homosexuality', *Psychiatric Quarterly*, 27 (1953) pp. 390–438.

Barker, J. C., 'Transsexualism and Transvestism', *Journal of the American Medical Association*, 198 (1966) p. 488.

Barlow, David H., Abel, Gene G. and Blanchard, Edward B., 'Gender Identity Change in Transsexuals', *Archives of General Psychiatry*, 36 (1979) pp. 1001–7.

Barlow, David H. and Agras, W. Stewart, 'Fading to Increase Heterosexual Responsiveness in Homosexuals', *Journal of Applied Behaviour Analysis*, 6, 3 (1973) pp. 355–66.

Barrett, Michèle, *Women's Oppression Today* (London: Verso, 1980).

Bastani, J. Boman and Kentsmith, David K., 'Psychotherapy with Wives of Sexual Deviants', *American Journal of Psychotherapy*, 34, 1 (1980) pp. 20–25.

Beigel, Hugo G. 'A Weekend in Alice's Wonderland', *Journal of Sex Research*, 5, 2 (1969) pp. 108–22.

Benjamin, Harry, 'Transvestism and Transsexualism', *International Journal of Sexology*, 7, 1 (1953) pp. 12–14.

Benjamin, Harry, *The Transsexual Phenomenon* (New York: Julian Press, 1966).

Benjamin, Harry, 'Transvestism and Transsexualism in the Male and Female', *Journal of Sex Research*, 3, 2 (1967) pp. 107–27.

Billings, Dwight B. and Urban, Thomas, 'The Socio-Medical Construction of Transsexualism: An Interpretation and Critique', *Social Problems*, 29, 3 (1982) pp. 266–82.

Bogdan, Robert, *Being Different: The Autobiography of Jane Fry* (New York: John Wiley, 1974).

Bond, I. K. and Evans, D. R., 'Avoidance Therapy: Its Use in Two Cases of Underwear Fetishism', *Canadian Medical Association Journal*, 96 (22 April 1967) pp. 1160–62.

Brake, Mike, 'I May Be a Queer, But At Least I am a Man: Male Hegemony and Ascribed versus Achieved Gender', in D. Leonard Barker and S. Allen (eds), *Sexual Divisions in Society: Process and Change* (London: Tavistock, 1976).

Brierley, H., *Transvestism: A Handbook with Case Studies for Psychologists, Psychiatrists and Counsellors* (Oxford: Pergamon Press, 1979).

Brown, Daniel G., 'Psychosexual Disturbances: Transvestism and Sex Role Inversion', *Marriage and Family Living*, 22 (1960) pp. 218–27.

Brown, Daniel G., 'Transvestism and Sex Role Inversion', in Albert Ellis and Albert Abarbanel (eds), *The Encyclopedia of Sexual Behaviour*, 2nd edn (New York: Hawthorn, 1967).

Buckner, H. Taylor, 'The Transvestic Career Path', *Psychiatry*, 33 (1970) pp. 381–9.

Buckner, H. Taylor, (ed.), *Deviance, Reality and Social Control* (New York: Random House, 1971).

Buhrich, N. 'A Heterosexual Transvestite Club: Psychiatric Aspects', *Australian and New Zealand Journal of Psychiatry* 10, 4 (1976) pp. 331–5.

Buhrich, N., 'A Case of Familial Heterosexual Transvestism', *Acta Psychiatrica et Neurologica Scandinavica*, 53, 3 (1977) pp. 199–201.

Buhrich, N., 'Motivation for Cross-dressing in Heterosexual Transvestism', *Acta Psychiatrica et Neurologica Scandinavica*, 57, 2 (1978) pp. 145–52.

Desavitsch, Eugene, *Homosexuality, Transvestism and Change of Sex* (London: Heinemann, 1958).

Echols, Alice, 'The New Feminism of Yin and Yang', in A. Snitow *et al.* (eds), *Desire: The Politics of Sexuality* (London: Virago, 1984).

Fallowell, Duncan and Ashley, April, *April Ashley's Odyssey* (London: Jonathan Cape, 1982).

Feinbloom, Deborah Heller, *Transvestites and Transsexuals* (USA: Delacorte Press, 1976).

Fenichel, Otto, *Collected Papers* (1st Series) (London: Routledge & Kegan Paul, 1954).

Fisk, Norman M., 'Gender Dysphoria Syndrome: the conception that liberalises indications for total gender reorientation and implies a broadly based multi-dimensional rehabilitative regimen', *Western Journal of Medicine*, 120 (May 1974) pp. 386–91.

Garfinkel, Harold, *Studies in Ethnomethodology* (New Jersey: Prentice Hall, 1967).

Gilbert, O. P., *Men in Women's Guise* (London: Bodley Head, 1926).

Gilbert, Sandra M., 'Costumes of the Mind: Transvestism as Metaphor in Modern Literature', in Elizabeth Abel (ed.), *Writing and Sexual Difference* (Brighton: Harvester Press, 1982).

Green, Richard, *Sexual Identity in Conflict in Children and Adults* (London: Duckworth, 1974).

Green, Richard, 'Sexual Identity of 37 Children Raised by Homosexual or Transsexual Parents', *American Journal of Psychiatry*, 135, 6 (1978) pp. 692–7.

Hamburger, Christian, Sturup, Georg K. and Dahl-Iversen, E., 'Transvestism: Hormonal, Psychiatric and Surgical Treatment', *Journal of the American Medical Association* 152, 5 (1953) pp. 391–6.

Jay, Monica, *Geraldine: For the Love of a Transvestite* (London: Caliban Books, 1985).

Jordan, Sandra, 'The Role of Counselling in Rehabilitation', in D. R. Laub and P. Gandy, (1973).

Kay, Barry, *The Other Women* (London: Matthews Miller Dunbar, 1976).

Kessler, Suzanne J. and McKenna, Wendy, *Gender: An Ethnomethodological Approach* (New York: John Wiley, 1978).

King, Dave, 'Gender Confusions: Psychological and Psychiatric Conceptions of Transvestism and Transsexualism', in Kenneth Plummer (ed.), *The Making of the Modern Homosexual* (London: Hutchinson, 1981).

King, Dave, 'Condition, Orientation, Role or False Consciousness? Models of Homosexuality and Transsexualism', *Sociological Review*, 32, 1 (1984) pp. 38–56.

King, Dave, 'Social Constructionism and Medical Knowledge: The Case of Transsexualism', *Sociology of Health and Illness*, 9, 4 (1987) pp. 352–77.

Kirk, Kris and Heath, Ed, *Men in Frocks* (London: GMP, 1984).

Langevin, Ron, 'The Meaning of Cross-Dressing', in Steiner (1985).

Langner, Lawrence, *The Importance of Wearing Clothes* (London: Constable, 1959).

Laub, Donald R. and Gandy, Patrick (eds), *Proceedings of the Second Interdisciplinary Symposium on Gender Dysphoria Syndrome* (Stanford: Stanford University Medical Centre, 1973).

Lurie, Alison, *The Language of Clothes* (Middlesex: Hamlyn, 1983).

Mackenzie, K. Roy, 'Gender Dysphoria Syndrome: Towards Standard Diagnostic Criteria', *Archives of Sexual Behaviour*, 7, 4 (1978) pp. 251–62.

McNeill, Sandra, 'Transsexualism . . . Can Men Turn Men into Women?', in S. Freedman and E. Sarah (eds), *On The Problem of Men* (London: Women's Press, 1982).

Maitland, Sara, *Vesta Tilley* (London: Virago, 1986).

Marcuse, Herbert, *Eros and Civilisation* (Boston: Beacon, 1965).

Masters, R. E. L., 'Transsexual Autobiographies', in Benjamin (1966).

Millett, Kate, *Sexual Politics* (London: Sphere, 1971).

Mitchell, Alison, 'The Politics of Cross-Dressing', *Glad Rag*, 34 (1987) pp. 19–20.

Money, John, 'Two Names, Two Wardrobes, Two Personalities', *Journal of Homosexuality*, 1, 1 (1974) pp. 65–70.

Newton, Esther, *Mother Camp: Female Impersonators in America* (Chicago: University of Chicago Press, 1972).

Nordyke, N. S., Baer, D. M., Etzel, B. C. and Leblanc, J. M.,

'Implications of the Stereotyping and Modification of Sex Role', *Journal of Applied Behaviour Analysis*, 10 (1977) pp. 553–7.

Pearce, James F., 'Aspects of Transvestism' (unpublished MD thesis, University of London, 1963).

Peo, Roger E., *Wives of Cross-Dressers: Isolated and Misunderstood* (Androgyny Unlimited, PO Box 4887, Poughkeepsie, NY 12602; no date).

Pepper, John, *A Man's Tale* (London: Quartet Books, 1982).

Person, Ethel and Ovesey, Lionel, 'Transvestism: New Perspectives', *Journal of the American Academy of Psychoanalysis*, 6, 3 (1978) pp. 301–23.

Plummer, Kenneth, *Documents of Life: An Introduction to the Problems and Literature of the Humanistic Method* (London: Allen & Unwin, 1983).

Polhemus, Ted and Proctor, Lynn, *Fashion and Anti-Fashion* (London: Thames & Hudson, 1978).

Pople, Martin, 'What Will You Wear to the Revolution?', *Marxism Today*, Jan (1987) pp. 44–5.

Prince, C. V., 'Homosexuality, Transvestism and Transsexualism', *American Journal of Psychotherapy*, 11, 1 (1957) pp. 80–85.

Prince, Virginia 'Charles', *The Transvestite and His Wife* (Los Angeles: Author, 1967).

Prince, V., 'Sex vs Gender', in D. Laub and P. Gandy (1973).

Prince, V., *Understanding Cross Dressing* (Los Angeles: Chevalier Publications, 1976).

Prince, Virginia and Bentler, P. M., 'Survey of 504 Cases of Transvestism', *Psychological Reports*, 31 (1972) pp. 903–17.

Randell, J. B., 'Transvestitism and Transsexualism', *British Medical Journal*, 2 (1959) p. 1448.

Randell, J. B., 'Transvestism and Transsexualism', *British Journal of Psychiatry Spec*, 9 (1975) pp. 201–5.

Raymond, Janice, 'Transsexualism: The Ultimate Homage to Sex Role Power', *Chrysalis*, 3 (1977).

Raymond, Janice G., *The Transsexual Empire* (London: Women's Press, 1980).

Redmount, Robert S., 'The Case of a Female Transvestite with Marital and Criminal Complications', *Journal of Clinical and Experimental Psychopathology*, 14, 2 (1953) pp. 95–111.

Rekers, G. A. and Lovaas, O. I., 'Behavioral Treatment of Deviant Sex-Role Behaviors in a Male Child', *Journal of Applied Behavior Analysis*, 7 (1974) pp. 173–90.

Richards, Janet Radcliffe, *The Sceptical Feminist: a philosophical enquiry* (Harmondsworth: Penguin 1982).

Riddell, Carol, *Divided Sisterhood: A Critical Review of Janice Raymond's 'The Transsexual Empire'* (Liverpool: News from Nowhere, 1980).

Segal, Morley M., 'Transvestism as an Impulse and as a Defence', *International Journal of Psychoanalysis*, 46 (1965) pp. 209–17.

Sinclair, Yvonne, *Transvestism Within a Partnership of Marriage and Families* (London: TV/TS Group, 1984).

Spector, Malcolm and Kitsuse, John I., *Constructing Social Problems* (California: Cummings Publishing, 1977).

Statham, June, *Daughters and Sons* (Oxford: Basil Blackwell, 1986).

Steiner, Betty W. (ed.), *Gender Dysphoria* (New York: Plenum Press, 1985).

Steiner, Betty W., 'The Management of Patients with Gender Disorders', in Steiner (1985).

Stoller, Robert J., 'Transvestites' Women', *American Journal of Psychiatry*, 124, 3 (1967) pp. 333–9.

Stoller, Robert J., *Sex and Gender* (New York: Science House, 1968).

Stoller, Robert J., 'The Term 'Transvestism'', *Archives of General Psychiatry*, 24, 3 (1971) pp. 230–37.

Stoller, Robert J., *Perversion: The Erotic Form of Hatred* (Sussex: Harvester, 1976).

Stoller, Robert J., 'Transvestism in Women', *Archives of Sexual Behaviour*, 11, 2 (1982) pp. 99–115.

Storr, Anthony, *Sexual Deviation* (Harmondsworth: Penguin, 1964).

Szasz, Thomas, *Ideology and Insanity* (London: Calder & Boyars, 1973).

Szasz, Thomas, *Sex: Facts, Frauds and Follies* (Oxford: Basil Blackwell, 1980).

Talamini, John T., *Boys Will be Girls* (Lanham Md: University Press of America, 1982).

Taylor, A. J. W. and McLachlan, D. G., 'Clinical and Psychological Observations on Transvestism', *New Zealand Medical Journal*, 61 (1962) pp. 496–502.

Taylor, A. J. W. and McLachlan, D. G., 'Further Observations and Comments on Transvestism', *New Zealand Medical Journal*, 62 (1963) pp. 527–9.

'Thompson, Janet', 'Transvestism: An Empirical Study', *International Journal of Sexology*, 4, 4 (1951) pp. 216–19.

Weeks, Jeffrey, *Sex, Politics and Society: The Regulation of Sexuality Since 1800* (London: Longman, 1981).

West, D. J., 'Thoughts on Sex Law Reform', in R. Hood (ed.), *Crime, Criminology and Public Policy* (London: Heinemann, 1974).

Wilson, Elizabeth, *Adorned in Dreams: Fashion and Modernity* (London: Virago, 1985).

Winkler, R. C., 'What Types of Sex-Role Behavior Should Behavior Modifiers Promote?, *Journal of Applied Behavior Analysis*, 10 (1977) pp. 549–52.

Wise, Thomas N., 'Psychotherapy of an Ageing Transvestite', *Journal of Sex and Marital Therapy*, 5, 4 (1979) pp. 368–73.

Wise, Thomas N., Dupkin, Carol and Meyer, Jon K., 'Partners of Distressed Transvestites', *American Journal of Psychiatry*, 138, 9 (1981) pp. 1221–4.

Wise, Thomas N. and Meyer, Jon K., 'Transvestism: Previous Findings and New Areas for Inquiry', *Journal of Sex and Marital Therapy*, 6, 2 (1980) pp. 116–28.

Wise, Thomas N. and Meyer, Jon K., 'The Border Area Between

Transvestism and Gender Dysphoria: Transvestite Applicants for Sex Reassignment', *Archives of Sexual Behaviour*, 9, 4 (1980) pp. 327–42.

Woodhouse, Ann, 'Forgotten Women: Transvestism and Marriage', *Women's Studies International Forum*, 8, 6 (1985) pp. 583–92.

Woodhouse, Annie, 'It's Okay for You to Wear the Trousers, But What If He Wants to Wear Your Skirts?', *Woman's World*, April (1987) pp. 116–17.

Woodhouse, Annie, 'Breaking the Rules or Bending Them? Transvestism, Femininity and Feminism', *Women's Studies International Forum* (1989).

Woolf, Virginia, *Orlando* (St Albans, Herts: Granada, 1977).

Yudkin, Marcia, 'Transsexualism and Women: A Critical Perspective', *Feminist Studies*, 4 (1978) pp. 97–106.

Zucker, Kenneth J., 'Cross-Gender-Identified Children', in Steiner (1985).

Index